UNEARTHING THE PAST

THE ARCHAEOLOGY OF THE FALLS OF THE OHIO RIVER REGION

DONALD E. JANZEN

ISBN 978-1-884532-95-5
Printed in Canada

Cover design by Scott Stortz

Published by:

Butler Books
P.O. Box 7311
Louisville, KY 40207
(502) 897-9393
Fax (502) 897-9797
www.butlerbooks.com

Historic photograph of the Falls of the Ohio River.
Courtesy of the Caufield & Shook Collection - CS.044303-O, Special Collections, University of Louisville

CONTENTS

Acknowledgments

It has been said that if you see a turtle sitting on the top of a fence post there is one thing you know for sure . . . it didn't get there all by itself. The same is true for this book and many people are responsible for its existence. First, thanks must be given to amateur archaeologists in the Falls of the Ohio River area. If it were not for people like Jim Matthews, Gene Atherton, John Vonderhaar, Clay Baird, and others, many important sites would have been destroyed without any artifacts to testify to their existence.

I was helped with many facets of this book, and in no order of importance, I wish to extend a sincere thanks to: Mr. Philip DiBlasi, Staff Archaeologist at the University of Louisville, for making collections from the KYANG site available for my inspection, and Denice Davis for helping me record information from the site artifact cards; Dr. George Lager of the Geology Department, University of Louisville, for his help in analyzing pottery from the Muddy Fork site; Mr. Leroy Koch, mussel biologist of the U.S. Fish & Wildlife Service for identifying a sample of freshwater mussels from the KYANG site; and to Katherine Horner, an anthropology student at the University of Louisville, for sharing with me information on her fieldwork in the Khanuy Valley of Central Mongolia.

Many people were gracious and let me photograph artifacts in their possession. Thanks to Edith Matthews for providing artifacts from the Clarksville, Minors Lane, and the Zorn Avenue sites; Mr. Stephen Mocas, the authority on ceramics from the Zorn Avenue site, for providing examples of pottery from this site; Larry Swan for the atlatl hook from the Lone Hill site, and John Vonderhaar (now deceased) for letting me photograph the axe he found at the Lone Hill site.

I would like to thank many people for providing me with photographs and drawings to use in this book. Thanks to Leigh Bader for doing all the drawings in the book; to Sue Finley of the Department of Special Collections, Ekstrom Library, University of Louisville, for researching and finding an historic photograph of the Falls of the Ohio River; the Louisville *Courier-Journal* for permission to use the photograph of Lone Hill, and the map of the Wet Woods; Anne Bader for permission to use her KYANG site engraved bone drawings that appeared in her University of Kentucky Master's thesis; Bear Soule for use of his personal photographs of the KYANG site excavations; Billy Davis (now deceased) for his interest in our excavations in 1969 and 1970, and for taking aerial photographs of the Clarksville site; and to Dick Burnett for photographing some of the artifacts that are shown in this book.

I have included present-day photographs of some of the areas where prehistoric sites were located and I wish to thank Ms. Judy Williams, Public Affairs Officer, for arranging with the Department of Veterans Affairs to have a photograph of the Zorn Avenue site taken from the roof of Louisville's Veteran's Hospital, and to William Stone for taking the photograph; and to the managers of Ruth's Chris Steak House for permission to photograph from the balcony of Kaden Tower.

I would like to thank Eugene Jaegers for proof reading the manuscript and reminding me where my language was too academic, and helping me put those pesky commas where they belonged.

I would especially like to thank Anne Bader for assisting me with this project every step of the way. It seems that at one time I borrowed every book in her library, and she directed me to literary sources that helped me tell this story. Her encouragement and assistance are greatly appreciated.

Foreword

This book has been in preparation for many years, but only in my mind. My excuse for the delay is that for the past thirty years I have been traveling across the country studying small cooperative communities and this is the first chance I have had to return to archaeology. Yes, this is a poor excuse.

I am going to begin this book with a chapter called, "Archaeology 101 for the Public." In describing archaeological sites there is no way to avoid using terminology and concepts that may be new to the reader. A description of topics like "developmental sequence" and "projectile point type" will be presented in what I hope is a clear and interesting way. The first chapter will also include a glossary of terms since archaeological terminology can sound like a foreign language. For some reason, either to make digging in dirt more respectable, or to impress granting agencies, archaeologists take simple concepts and describe them in confusing ways. For example, if you told the average first or second grader that Native Americans got flint and chipped tools from it they would understand the process. To the archaeologist it never happened this way. First, Native Americans never "got" anything, they "procured" it. Furthermore, Native Americans carried this one step further and had a "procurement strategy". I guess this is to imply that they didn't wander randomly around the countryside, although I suspect that few cultural groups ever did this. Now we can't use the word "flint" because technically this refers to a special kind of silicon dioxide, and in most cases what was used for tool making was an impure variety called chert. All right, didn't Native Americans chip tools from chert? No, they put the chert through a reduction process. So, we now tell our first and second graders that Native Americans had procurement strategies for obtaining chert and made tools by putting it through a reduction process. Wow! I have attempted to strip this kind of language from my vocabulary and "procurement strategy" will be replaced with the word "plan".

I have also included a chapter on the physical setting of the Falls of the Ohio region. The reader may not be aware that within a thirty mile radius of Louisville, there is more geographical diversity that anywhere else in Kentucky. This diversity translated into an ideal place for Native Americans to live, and state records show there are over 600 known archaeological sites in just Jefferson County. Because of industrial and residential development in Louisville, and the cities across the Ohio River, the vast majority of these sites are now gone. The eight sites described in this book are intended to give the reader a sampling of the area's prehistory. I have selected sites that have been either totally destroyed, or are on property where there are laws that prohibit digging for artifacts. I did not want to mention sites still in existence and encourage trespassing on private property.

I suspect that some readers will be knowledgeable amateur archaeologists, or people who may have had a course in archaeology. For these people, the discussion will occasionally be more detailed. Actually, archaeology is not rocket science, so anyone with an interest should be able to grasp more complex concepts.

I have intentionally not included bibliographic references in the text of this book, but there is a list of references by chapter at the end of the book. Here, I have commented on each reference to give some background about the book or article.

I hope that the reader will find reading about the prehistory of the Falls of the Ohio area interesting and will learn something about how the archaeologist approaches an understanding of past cultures.

Archaeology 101 for the Public

The purpose of this chapter is to introduce the reader to some of the ABC's of archaeology. One way to think about archaeology is to view it as having three dimensions; time, space, and culture.

The Dimension of Time

One of the first jobs of the archaeologist when excavating a site is to date when it was occupied. By knowing the age of sites it is possible to establish chronologies and propose ways that prehistoric cultures developed over time. The concept of stratigraphy (horizontal layering) is used to determine the relative dates of cultural deposits with the lower deposits being older that the upper ones. If there are any organic remains at a site, such as charcoal from a fire pit, it can be given an absolute date using radiocarbon dating. In some cases it is not possible to obtain material for carbon-14 dating, but artifacts are recovered that are similar to those found on another site that has been dated. In this case the archaeologist assumes that similar artifacts have broadly similar dates. This technique is called cross-dating.

The Dimension of Space

Archaeological sites are distributed in geographical space and the spread of new ideas, such as pottery making and plant domestication, do not occur everywhere at the same time, but originate in a geographical area and then spread to new ones. In regions where there appears to be uniformity in the physical setting, archaeologists will lump sites together and refer to the prehistory of the Upper Great Lakes, or Lower Ohio Valley. Sometimes archaeologists consider smaller geographical areas, and in the case of the Falls of the Ohio River region, geographers have defined five unique zones, or physiographic provinces. These will be discussed in detail in the next chapter.

The Dimension of Culture

In the United States, archaeologists are trained as anthropologists and their main goal is to reconstruct the culture of prehistoric people. One way this is done is to study the subsistence and settlement patterns. The diet can be inferred by analyzing animal bone from trash pits, and dissolving samples of soil for charred plant remains. Prior to agriculture, people were nomadic and often scheduled their movements to coincide with the seasons and the availability of plants and animals. By analyzing the food remains at a site the archaeologist attempts to reconstruct these seasonal movements.

When house patterns are preserved, it is possible to infer if people lived in single family units, or perhaps extended families. An analysis of artifacts associated with burials, especially the kinds of artifacts and their numbers, can give clues about the status of an individual and if there was social stratification within the group.

Archaeological Data - What the Archaeologist Observes

When archaeologists excavate a site, what they observe can be classified into five different categories of data. It is this data that is used to place sites into a temporal framework and to reconstruct the culture of its inhabitants.

What the Archaeologist Observes

1 - Artifacts

2 - Non-Artifacts

3 - Features

4 - Associations

5 - Quantities

1 - Artifacts - An artifact is an object that someone has modified in one of the following ways:

    a) Deliberate shaping - a chipped stone tool, a clay pottery vessel,
        a mussel shell bead
    b) Application - a stone, bone, or cave wall that has had pigment
        applied to it
    c) Simple use - an unmodified stone that has been altered by using
        it as a hammer or an abrader

2 - Non-Artifacts - It is assumed that these items are found in the context of an archaeological site. Non-artifacts can be divided into two categories:

a) Materials that are the by-product of human activity

    I. Chippage debris - the waste flakes from chipping a stone tool
    ii. Animal bones - food remains
    iii. Plant remains - charred nut shells
    iv. Fire-cracked rock - fractured rocks that lined a fire pit

b) Materials that provide data about prehistoric environments

    I. Snails (these are good climate indicators)
    ii. Fossil pollens
    iii. Soil pH and composition
    iv. Silts and sands indicating the location of past rivers
    and streams and evidence of past floods

3 - Features - Features are complexes of two or more artifacts and/or non-artifacts. Examples are:

    a) Caches of artifacts
    b) Stones arranged around a fire pit
    c) Post molds - dark stains from decaying posts that were part of a structure
    d) A burial mound
    e) Workshop areas where stone tools were flaked

The most significant aspect of a feature is its association with artifacts and non-artifacts.

4 - Associations - The spatial proximity of artifacts and non-artifacts, as well as the association of sites with features of the environment, such as lakes, streams, upland areas, rockshelters, and caves. The archaeologist relies on associations for such things as:

    a) Absolute dating - charcoal associated with a fire pit can be subjected to radiocarbon dating and give a date for the fire pit and any artifacts associated with it
    b) Relative dating - the stratigraphic relationship of artifacts, non-artifacts and features with the upper deposits being more recent than the lower ones
    c) Settlement pattern - site location in relation to physical features of the environment

5 - Quantities - Artifacts, non-artifacts, and features can be counted and a quantity established. From this the archaeologist can infer:

    a) Status - the number of grave goods associated with a burial can be used to infer the status of this individual in the society
    b) Diet - by counting the number of animal bones (deer, small mammal, fish, and fowl) it is possible to reconstruct the relative importance of these items in the diet
    c) Cultural preferences - by counting the different kinds of stone used in making tools it is possible to infer the preferred source of raw material
    d) Site occupation - the number of artifacts recovered from a site can be used as an indication of its length, or frequency, of occupancy

These five items are what the archaeologist observes. Note that the archaeologist does not directly observe human cultural behavior but the manifestations of this behavior. The reconstruction of prehistoric cultures is therefore based on inferences made from artifacts, non-artifacts, features, associations, and quantities.

Kinds of Archaeological Evidence

Not all archaeological evidence is the same, and inferences based on some kinds of evidence have a higher degree of validity than others.   It is useful to think of archaeological evidence as being divided into three classes.

Kinds of Archaeological Evidence

1 - Empirical or observable evidence

2 - Logical evidence

3 - Speculative or intuitive evidence

1 - Empirical or Observable Evidence

This kind of evidence is (1) artifacts, (2) non-artifacts, (3) features, (4) associations, and (5) quantities. Not all empirical evidence is equally valid and inferences based on whole artifacts are better that ones based on fragments. Dates based on counting tree rings have a higher degree of validity than radiocarbon dates.

2 - Logical Evidence

If empirical evidence is absent, it is possible to base inferences on logic. Direct evidence of domesticated grain, or the use of wild plant seeds, may be absent from a site, but the present of milling stones can be used to logically infer that these were part of the diet. Another kind of logical evidence is using what archaeologists call "Ethnographic Analogy." This examines cultural practices of present-day cultures, such as the kinds of social organization among hunters and gatherers, and logically assumes that such groups had similar kinds of practices in the past. Inferences based on logical evidence have a lower degree of validity than those based on empirical or observable evidence.

3 - Speculative or Intuitive Evidence

This kind of evidence cannot be used as proof, or disproof, and has the lowest degree of reliability. The voyage of the Kon Tiki demonstrated that ancient Peruvians could have sailed to islands in the Pacific. It did not prove they did.

Culture and Environment

All cultures exist in a physical environment and rely on it for food and natural resources. Early geographers studied the interaction between cultures and their environment and postulated that the environment dictated the nature of the culture. This was called "Environmental Determinism." Anthropologists recognize that while the environment can place limitations on cultures, it does not preordain its structure. Today, the interplay between the environment and the technology of a culture is called Cultural Ecology.

Cultural Ecology

Cultural ecology is the study of social groups and how they structure their society to exploit various environments with the technologies available to them.

Environmental Limitations

The environment places restraints on cultures and often limitations on the availability of natural resources. For example, in the expansion of prehistoric corn horticulture, the early variety required 120 frost-free days to mature. Although Native Americans living in northern areas might know about corn, the climate made agriculture ineffective and hunting and gathering remained the major subsistence base.

Cultural Limitations

Although the environment might have natural resources that could benefit prehistoric populations, their technology placed restraints on the degree to which these resources could be exploited. The plains area of the United States had favorable soils for growing corn, however, native groups in this area did not have metallurgy and used bone tools to cultivate the ground (the shoulder blade - scapula of a bison). These bone hoes could not pierce the tough plains grasses so farming had to be restricted to river bottoms where the soil was easily worked. When Europeans arrived they had the steel plow and converted the plains states into the breadbasket of the country.

Native Americans inhabited the New World during times when the environment was difference from what it is today. For example, streams and lakes that were in existence 5,000 years ago may have been important locations for prehistoric settlements. The archaeologist must therefore gather data to reconstruct such past environments as a background for interpreting artifacts, non-artifacts, features, associations, and quantities.

Prehistoric Developmental Sequence for the Eastern United States

One of the important jobs of the archaeologist is to take the continuum of time and divide it into segments. This makes it possible to compare data from different time periods and propose hypotheses about prehistoric cultural development. The criteria used to define these stages are artifacts, non-artifacts, and features that seem to indicate that a major cultural change has occurred. The developmental sequence for the Eastern United States consists of four periods with two of these divided into an Early, Middle, and Late Phase. The date for the start and end of these phases varies according to location since it takes time for cultural changes to spread over geographical areas. The following dates for these phases are the best estimates for the Falls of the Ohio River region.

Paleo-Indian Period (12,000 - 8,000 B.C.)

The Paleo-Indian Period refers to the first peopling of the Americas and archaeologists believe this occurred no earlier than 20,000 years ago. This was during the last glacial period when sea levels were lowered and groups could cross a land bridge from Asia over what is now the Bering Strait. Climatic conditions were different from those of today and animals now extinct, such as mammoths and mastodons, still roamed the countryside. These first people were hunters and gatherers, probably highly nomadic, and lived in small groups. The diagnostic artifact that defines this period is a leaf-shaped spear point with a flute, or groove, running along the main axis of the artifact on both sides. Although these points are rare, they have been found in the Falls of the Ohio River area.

Paleo-Indian fluted projectile point
(From Richard M. Burnett collection)

Archaic Period (8,000 -1,000 B.C.)

The Archaic period starts around 8,000 B.C., and by this time glacial ice had retreated into Canada. Climatic conditions were now approaching those of the present and there was increasing environmental diversity. As this occurred Native Americans adapted ways of efficiently exploiting these new environments for food and natural resources. Groups were now able to live in larger numbers, and in places where there were abundant plant and animal resources, they may have stayed most of the year. In fact, the Falls of the Ohio River region may have been one of these places where thriving plant and animal populations could support sedentary living for hunters and gathers.

Since the Archaic period spans 7,000 years, archaeologist have divided it into an Early, Middle, and Late phase to better understand the changes that were taking place. The artifact inventory was highly diversified with a variety of stemmed and notched spear points replacing the Paleo-Indian fluted point. Other chipped stone tools included drills, gravers, and various kinds of scraping tools. Ground stone tools, such as grooved axes and pestles were made and bone was used to fashion needles, and awls, and items of personal adornment such as beads.

Woodland Period
Early Woodland   (1,000 B.C. - 200 B.C.)

The Woodland Period, like the Archaic, is divided into an Early, Middle, and Late phase. The Early Woodland starts around 1,000 B.C. and has three main defining criteria; the beginnings of plant domestication, settled village life, and ceramic making. This is the period that is commonly called "The Mound Builders." Squash, and later beans and maize, originally domesticated in Mexico, find their way to North America and produce a profound change in Native American life. Instead of a nomadic life spent chasing game and exploiting seasonal wild plant communities, plant domestication allows food sources to be brought to the group. Horticulture can produce surpluses and this frees people to pursue other activities. There is now a suggestion of craft specialization and social stratification is reflected in the construction of earthen burial mounds for an elite minority.

A particularly elaborate form of Early Woodland culture, known as Adena, developed in south central Ohio and extended southeast to Charleston, West Virginia and southwest to the Lexington, Kentucky area. A site that yielded many of the diagnostic artifacts of this culture has been found in the Louisville area.

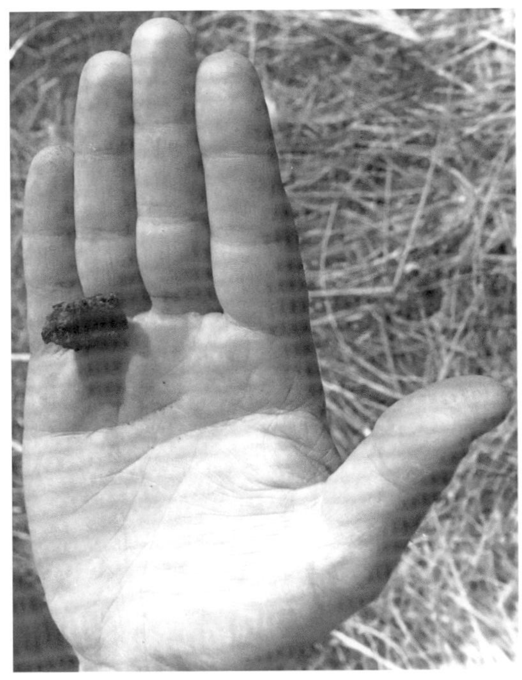

Charred prehistoric corn cob from a site in southwestern Jefferson County, Kentucky

Middle Woodland   (200 B.C. - A.D.500)

The Middle Woodland period begins around 200 B.C. and is an elaboration and intensification of cultural practices started in the Early Woodland. Plant domestication plays a more important role in the subsistence pattern and artifacts associated with the dead in mounds become more elaborate and display a high level of craftsmanship. The height of Middle Woodland development occurs in Ohio and Illinois with the Hopewell culture. There is evidence of long-distance trade of items such as; marine shell from the Atlantic and Gulf coasts of Florida, copper from the Upper Great Lakes, mica from the Appalachians, and obsidian from Yellowstone Park. Native Americans in Kentucky appear to have been on the fringes of Hopewellian influence and continued to expand on an Early Woodland way of life.

Late Woodland (A.D. 500 - Historic)

The Late Woodland period begins around A.D. 500 and ends with European contact. Some archaeologists are now ending the Late Woodland at A.D. 1,000 and adding Late Prehistoric as the final period. It is during the Late Woodland that the bow is introduced into Eastern North America. What we today call "arrowheads" were actually spears and this is why archaeologists call them "projectile points." True arrow points are usually about an inch long and are triangular in shape.

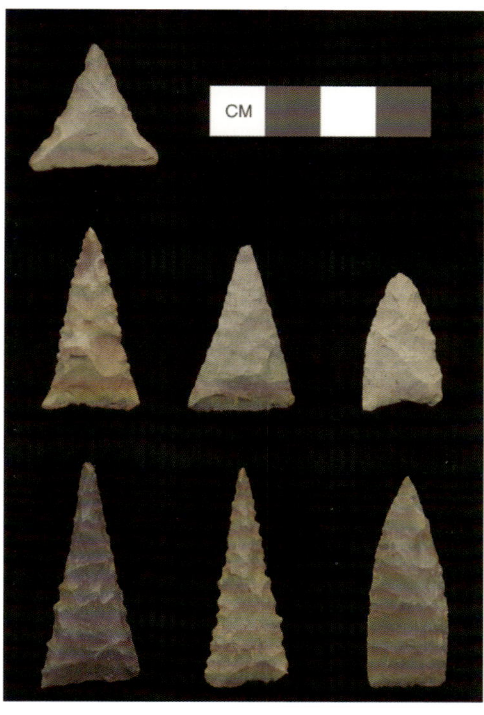

Arrow points from sites in the Falls area

During the Late Woodland period agriculture becomes more developed. Villages start out small, but grow in size as maize, beans and squash take a more prominent role in the diet. The elaborate mortuary practices of the Early and Middle Woodland periods fade away. This might appear to be a cultural regression, but that may not be the case. Ritual centers always seem more exciting than small farming communities.

Although the Late Woodland / Late Prehistoric period ends with European contact, it is difficult to correlate sites and artifacts with particular Native American tribes described by early settlers of the area. There are accounts indicating that the Shawnee were in Kentucky and their ancestors may have been the ones who inhabited some to the late period sites in the Falls area.

Mississippian (A.D. 1,000 - Historic)

In the Southeastern United States and along the Mississippi River and its major tributaries, an elaborate culture develops around A.D. 1,000 that is called Mississippian. Large centers with flat-topped, pyramidal mounds are build and the social and political life is controlled by powerful chiefs. Agriculture reaches a level where it is able to support settlements that are large enough to be called urban centers. The Cahokia site near East St. Louis is an example of such a center. This appears to have been a turbulent time because there is evidence of human sacrifice and warfare. There is evidence of palisaded walls built for protection against invaders. One of the characteristic artifacts of Mississippian culture is pottery with crushed mussel shell used as a temper.

The largest known Mississippian site in the Ohio Valley is the Angle Mounds near Evansville, Indiana. The Falls of the Ohio River appear to have been the upstream limit of Mississippian expansion, or influence. In this area the archaeological record suggests an overlap of Late Woodland/Late Prehistoric and Mississippian cultures. Unfortunately, many sites that could have shed light on the interaction between these two groups have been destroyed with the development of Louisville and its suburbs.

Classification

Once the archaeologist has collected data (artifacts, non-artifacts, features, associations, and determined the quantities of these) one of the first steps is to classify what has been found. Classification serves several purposes:

1 - to bring order to the collection
2 - to assist in describing the collection
3 - to assist in making comparisons

There are two main ways the data can be classified.

Descriptive Classification

This is a description of the form or shape of the artifact, non-artifact, or feature. An artifact might be classified as "a notched, bifacially worked tool", which is an objective, accurate description of the tool. Two frequently used descriptive types are:

Bifacial tool - a tool where both sides of a flake have been chipped
Unifacial tool - a tool where only one side of a flake has been chipped

Functional Classification

This kind of classification assumes the function of the artifact is known. Instead of "a notched, bifacially worked tool" the artifact would be classified as a "projectile point". The assumption is that it was secured to the end of a shaft which was used as a spear or a lance. Problems can arise with functional classifications since an alternate use might be possible. Perhaps the "notched, bifacially worked tool" was secured to a handle and used as a knife.

In writing up the artifact inventory from a site, the archaeologist will sort the collection into a hierarchy of categories based on both a descriptive and functional classification.

I. CHIPPED STONE ARTIFACTS
    Bifacial Artifacts
        Projectile points
        Drills
    Unifacial Artifacts
        End scrapers
        Side scrapers

II. GROUND STONE ARTIFACTS
    Axes
    Pestles

III. BONE AND ANTLER ARTIFACTS
    Awls
    Needles
    Fishhooks

IV. CERAMICS
    Cord-marked sherds
    Plain sherds

V. SHELL
    Beads

Projectile Point Typology

Perhaps the most important artifact that helps the archaeologist understand the dimensions of time, space, and culture, is the projectile point. Usually Native Americans followed prescribed cultural standards for the size and shape of a point and these changed over time and across geographical space. The projectile point therefore serves as a kind of prehistoric calling card for telling the archaeologist where people have been and when they were there.

The archaeologist classifies projectile points into types and begins this process by breaking the artifact into its component parts called attributes.

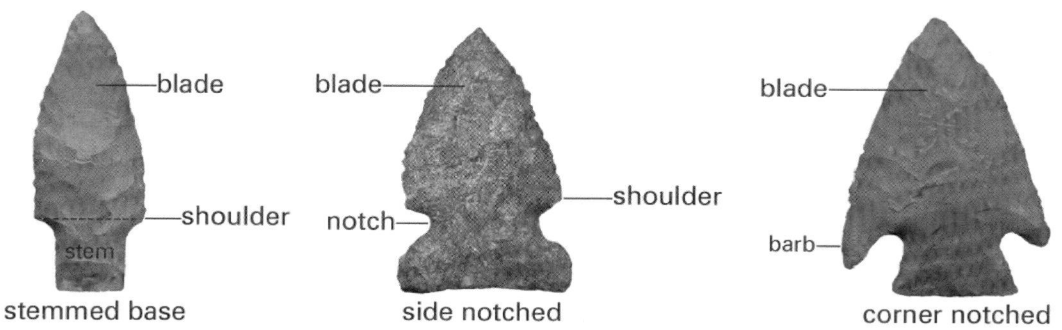

THE ANATOMY OF A PROJECTILE POINT

The Anatomy of a Projectile Point shown above identifies some of the major attributes, but archaeologists usually refine these and also describe such things as the curvature of the blade and base and the shape of the stem. Attributes can also be measured, such as the length of the point or the width of the shoulder, and these are called "metric attributes." When a group of projectile points share a cluster of attributes they are classified into a type and given a name. Often projectile points will have similar configurations but their measurements are vastly different. In these cases the metric attributes are important in distinguishing between two different types.

In many cases a particular projectile point style will occur over a large geographical area and be given different type names. For example, archaeologists working in Alabama and Tennessee gave the name Bakers Creek to a group of projectile points that had (among other attributes) triangular blades and flared bases. Archaeologists working in Illinois called projectile points with similar attributes Lowe Flared Base. There is justification for doing this because the two areas are some distance apart, and if they were given the same name the implication would be that they were made by the same people. Archaeologists do not like to make these kind of implications based solely on projectile point styles. The problem is that the geographical distributions of these two types overlap and both include the entire state of Kentucky. In these situations, the author has relied on an excellent book by Noel Justice (see bibliography) for classifying projectile points, and hopes the knowledgeable reader will forgive the author if he selects one type name over another.

Projectile Point Types from the Falls of the Ohio River Region

Thebes
8000-6000 B.C.

St. Charles
8000-6000 B.C.

Kirk Serrated
6900-6000 B.C.

Matanza
3700-2200 B.C.

McWhinney
4000-1000 B.C.

Merom
Expanding Stem
1600-1000 B.C.

Buck Creek Barbed
1500-600 B.C.

Wade
1000-500 B.C.

Adena Stemmed

800-300 B.C.

Lowe
Flared Base
A.D. 200-600

Jack's Reef
Corner Notched
A.D. 800-1200

Madison

A.D. 800 - historic

Glossary of Archaeological Terms

Absolute date - A date that can be correlated with the Christian calendar. Radiocarbon dating is the most common kind of absolute dating.

Bifacial tool - A stone tool that has been chipped on two opposing surfaces. An example would be a projectile point or drill.

Blank - see Preform

Celt - A ground stone tool resembling an axe but without a groove. This tool was probably used in woodworking.

Chert - The name of an impure variety of flint that was extensively used to make chipped stone tools. Several different varieties of chert naturally occur in the Falls of the Ohio River region.

Component - This refers to the occupation of an archaeological site during a specific time period. A site that was inhabited only during the Archaic period would be called a "single component" site, while a multi-component site would be one inhabited, for instance, during both the Archaic and Early Woodland periods.

Cord-marked pottery - Pottery that has the impressions of twisted fibers on it. These were made by patting the wet clay with a paddle wrapped with fiber cords. The purpose of this was to smooth the area between the coils of clay and remove air bubbles.

Core - The interior of a chunk of chert that has been used to make chipped stone tools. A core can be thought of as the waste product after flakes have been removed from a piece of chert.

Cortex - The exterior portion of a stone that has been chemically altered by weathering. The first step in making a chipped stone tool is to remove the cortex.

Celt

Core

Chert flake with cortex
exterior

Drill

Fire-cracked rock

Cross dating - This is a kind of relative dating where a site is dated by comparing artifacts with similar ones from a site that has an absolute date (see Absolute Date).

Culture - The learned, shared behavioral patterns of a group of people

Drill - A bifacially worked tool that has an elongated tip that resembles a drill bit. The exact function of these tools is not known but they were probably used to drill holes in wood, bone, or antler.

Fire-cracked rock -   A rock that displays cracks and fractures as a result of being heated. It is assumed that fire cracked rocks lined fire pits.

Ground stone tool -   These tools were usually fashioned from river cobbles by using a hammerstone to shape the tool, and then other stones to grind it into its final form.   The most common ground stone tools are axes, celts, and pestles.

Hafted scraper - The word "haft" refers to a hilt or handle. Hafted scrapers are scraping tools that were secured to a handle. It is assumed that these handles were usually made of wood, bone, or antler.   It appears that hafted scrapers were made from broken projectile points where the tip was reworked into a scraper.

Hammerstone - These were usually golf ball to tennis ball-sized water-worn pebbles that were used as a hammer. Hammerstones are identified since the battering removed a portion of the weathered exterior of the stone and exposed the lighter colored interior.

Midden - This refers to a soil layer that is the result of human habitation. The soil is usually of a darker color than native soils of the area, and is composed of prehistoric refuse, fire-cracked rocks, and artifacts. Animal bone and shell fragments can also be associated with midden deposits.

Preform - A bifacially worked tool that has not been completely finished into its final form. These are often called "blanks" and were made with the intention that they would eventually be fashioned into a projectile point, knife, or some other implement.

Projectile point - A pointed, bifacially flaked tool that was used as a spear or lance tip. Although the term projectile point implies the function of the artifact, it is possible that some of these tools were attached to a handle and used as a knife.

Relative date - This is a comparative date simply stating that something is older or more recent than something else.   The most common method of relative dating used by archaeologists is stratigraphy where the lowest deposits are assumed to be older than the upper ones.

Sherd - A fragment or broken piece of pottery

Temper - Material added to the potter's clay to help bond a vessel together after it is fired. Common tempers used by Native Americans were crushed stone (grit), sand and crushed mussel shells.

Unifacial tool - A chipped stone tool that has been worked (chipped) on only one face or side of a flake. Most scraping tools were manufactured in this way.

Workshop site - A site where the primary function was to take raw material (usually chert) and make tools. Often only the initial stages of tool making (manufacturing preforms for example) were done at a workshop site.

Hafted Scrapers

Hammerstone

Preform

Physical Setting

If you are like most people, you will either skim over this chapter, or ignore it completely. When the author first started reading archaeological site reports, the descriptions of the physical settings were usually boring and they seemed to be included more as an academic exercise than anything else. Often this turned out to be the case since the ensuing report seldom related the finding of the excavations back to the physical setting. The author hopes to convince the reader that this will not be the case here. A knowledge of the physical setting of the Falls region is important in understanding and interpreting the prehistoric occupation of the area.

It was only when the author started directing archaeological excavations in the Falls area in 1969, and studied the region's flora, fauna, geology, and physical geography, that he truly gained an appreciation of its diversity. I grew up in Louisville and thought I knew a lot about Jefferson and the adjacent counties. I sailed on the Ohio River, had birthday parties at Big Rock in Cherokee Park, enjoyed productions at the amphitheater in Iroquois Park, went to Standiford Field airport, and drove up Muldraugh Hill to Fort Knox when I was in the army. I had no idea at the time that these excursions were taking me through five distinct zones, or as physical geographers call them, physiographic provinces. The names assigned to these provinces are:

The Alluvial Plain of the Ohio River
The Outer Blue Grass
The Scottsburg Lowland
The Knobs
The Mississippian Plateaus

The first four of these zones are present in Jefferson County, and the fifth (The Mississippian Plateaus) can be found in adjacent Hardin County, and in central Harrison County, Indiana. No where else in the state of Kentucky can such geographical (and environmental) diversity be found compressed into one area. Although not classified as a separate geographical zone, the Falls of the Ohio River was certainly a unique ecological niche and in prehistoric times may have been unmatched in the Eastern United States for its diversity of aquatic life. It should be mentioned that the classification of geographical regions is done on a state-by-state basis. In Indiana the Outer Blue Grass is called the Muscatatuck Regional Slope, and the Knobs are referred to as the Norman Upland. That portion of the Mississippian Plateaus downstream from the Falls in Indiana is the Mitchell Plain. Only the Scottsburg Lowland name is the same in both states.

Now, into this setting of five physiographic provinces and the Falls, place prehistoric people. Diverse environments mean that there are diverse natural resources, and so native populations didn't have to go far to find a variety of different foods and materials essential to their livelihood. Let's explore these physiographic provinces and see what natural resources they provided prehistoric people.

The Alluvial Plain of the Ohio River

Most of the Ohio River owes its origin to glaciers. During the last ice age, the advancing glacier dammed the drainage

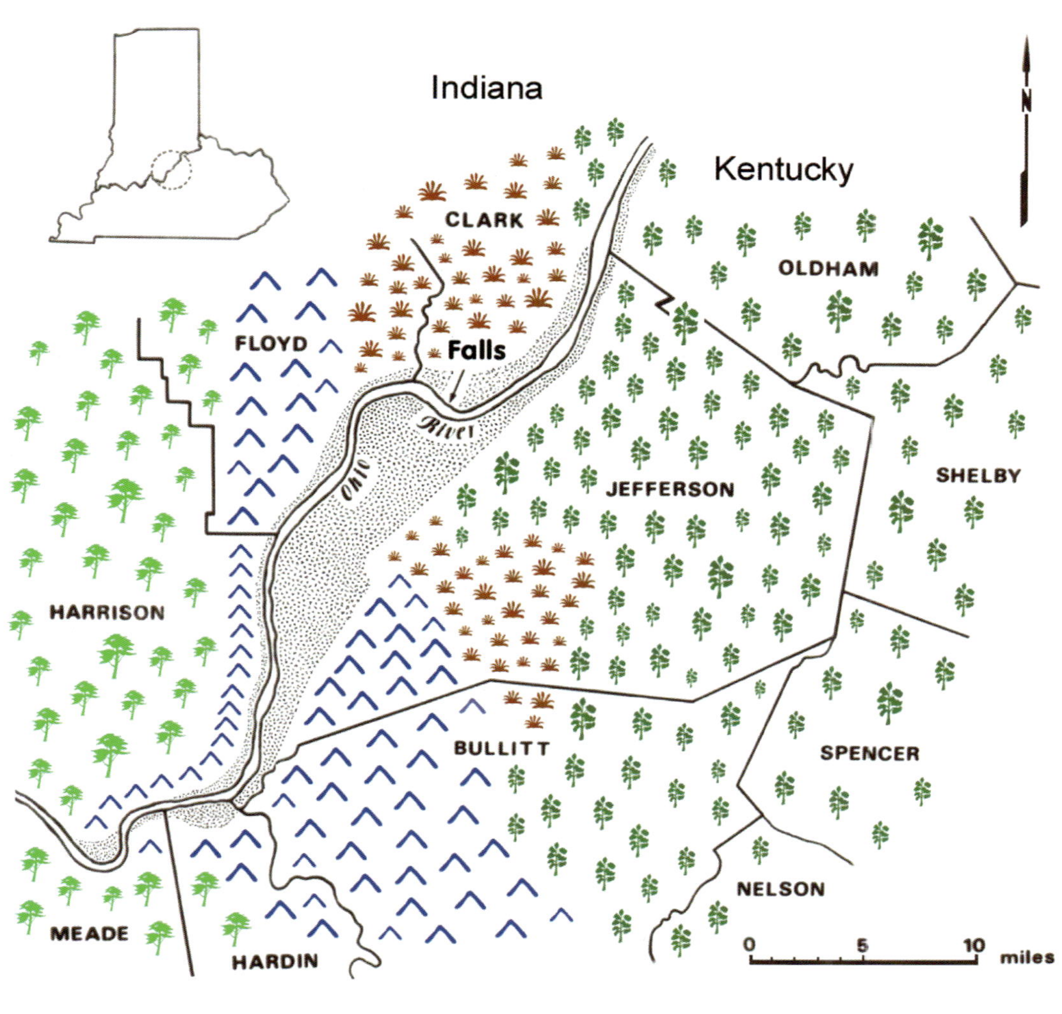

KENTUCKY	INDIANA
Outer Blue Grass	Muscatatuck Regional Slope
Scottsburg Lowland	Scottsburg Lowland
Knobs	Norman Upland
Mississippian Plateau	Mitchell Plain
Ohio River Flood Plain	Ohio River Flood Plain

Physiographic Provinces in the Falls of the Ohio River Region

patterns of the then northwesterly flowing streams, like the Kentucky and Licking Rivers. When the glacier started melting, a series of lakes were formed along its southern margins. As these lakes grew in size their runoff sought new routes and eventually they were connected with a common drainage system. With the retreat of the glacier the melting water followed this route, cutting a deep channel and creating the Lower Ohio River. In one area, as the river continued to down-cut, it encountered bedrock. The result was a break in the flow of the river and the development of a series of rapids that became known as the Falls of the Ohio River. Today the Ohio River has been drastically altered by the construction of a series of locks and dams and the Falls, as well as several small islands, are now submerged.

It is difficult for us to imagine today the abundance of wildlife, such as fish, aquatic birds, deer, elk and other animals that must have existed at the Falls of the Ohio during prehistoric times. A number of famous 19th century naturalists such as Constantine Rafinesque, Thomas Say, Isaac Lea and Ellsworth Call were drawn to the Falls to study the fish, snail and mussel populations. It must have been an ideal outdoor laboratory because numerous species were first identified at the Falls. Many of the early descriptions of

Looking south down the Ohio River with the flood plain in Jefferson County, Kentucky, on the left, and the Knobs Escarpment in Harrison County, Indiana, on the right. Behind the knobs is the Mitchell Plain. (© *The Courier-Journal*)

fish are so amazing that if it were not for supporting accounts, they would be considered the product of the kind of exaggeration so frequently associated with "fish stories." There were suckers and freshwater drum three feet in length, and catfish and sturgeon that weighed 30 to 100 pounds, and some that exceeded 200 pounds. (Some early accounts are given in Daniel F. Jackson; see bibliography).

Fresh water molluscan fauna (snails and mussels) were present in great abundance and massive mussel beds existed in shallow portions of the river. These must have been an important part of the diet of the prehistoric inhabitants because over the centuries the discarded shells created literal mountains. On the Ohio River near Addison, Kentucky (in Breckinridge County), there is a shell heap so large that the Corps of Engineers was able to build houses on top of it.

The Outer Bluegrass - Muscatatuck Regional Slope

Kentucky is known as the Bluegrass State and this is derived from the rolling grasslands in the central part of the state. The central part of the province is called the Inner Bluegrass and as it spreads out the margins are referred to as the Outer Bluegrass. The terrain is gently rolling hills and Seneca and Cherokee Parks are excellent examples of the Outer Bluegrass in the Louisville area. Across the Ohio River in Indiana this province is called the Muscatatuck Regional Slope. Numerous streams, such as Floyds Fork, the three forks of Beargrass Creek, and Harrods Creek drain the Outer Bluegrass in the Louisville area.   In Indiana, Fourteen Mile Creek is a well-known drainage since it helps define a famous ridge called the Devil's Backbone. These streams served as prehistoric highways for easy access from the Ohio

The Outer Bluegrass in eastern Jefferson County, Kentucky

River to inland areas. Game such as deer and perhaps elk were an important prehistoric food resource in the Outer Bluegrass and clays were utilized when the knowledge of ceramic making was obtained.

The Scottsburg Lowland

The Scottsburg Lowland is a sizable physiographic province in Indiana that starts in Johnson County and runs southward to the flood plain of the Ohio River. A remnant of the Scottsburg Lowland is present in Jefferson County and northern Bullitt County, but it is so small that it has not been given province status. Often it is classified as a subdivision of the Outer Bluegrass, but it is a unique geographical zone in Kentucky. The most prominent landmark in this area today is the Louisville airport, Standiford Field. What makes the Scottsburg Lowland distinctive is its bedrock. Limestone is the prevailing bedrock in the Falls area, but the Scottsburg Lowland is underlain with shale. Limestone can be dissolved by slightly acidic water, as testified by sinkholes and caves, but water is unable to drain through shale. The result is an area that is wet and can become swampy, in fact, early maps of this portion of Jefferson County refer to it as the Wet Woods. To correct this condition, the Northern and Southern Ditches were created to drain the area. What makes the Kentucky Scottsburg Lowland important to the archaeologist is the massive prehistoric sites that have been found in this area. All of these sites fall within the time period of 3,000 to 1,000 B.C. and represent pre-agricultural people who were hunters and gathers.

Archaeologists do not know what attracted prehistoric people to the Scottsburg Lowland, but the answer may have to do with vegetation. In the 1950s, Charles Gunn did a study of the plants in Jefferson and the seven adjacent counties and referred to those in the Kentucky Scottsburg Lowland as ". . . unique to this area of Kentucky." This is an amazing

Looking south at the Kentucky Scottsburg Lowland from the Knobs near Fairdale

statement considering the small area that the Lowland covers in the state. Whether it was the plants, or the wildlife that was drawn to these plants, the Kentucky Scottsburg Lowland provided a resource that attracted prehistoric people to the area.

The Knobs - Norman Upland

The Knobs of Kentucky, and Norman Upland in Indiana, are a series of low, conical hills that rise abruptly to the west and south of the Scottsburg Lowland, and are an easily recognizable natural region. They are defined by a continuous escarpment that starts in Brown County, Indiana, runs southward to the Ohio River, continues in Kentucky in Jefferson County, runs south, turns east through Bullitt and Lincoln Counties, and then bends north to Lewis County in Northern Kentucky. In places the Knobs rise 400 or 500 feet above the Scottsburg Lowland and are drained by deeply cut streams. Some of these streams have carved large rock overhangs, or rock shelters, which appear to have been favorite habitation places during prehistoric times. One of the natural resources of the Knobs is a low grade iron ore called siderite. This was utilized by the early settlers of the area and in Bullitt County the remains of several iron furnaces are still visible. Native Americans used this material to make ground stone tools such as pestles and axes.

The Mississippian Plateau - Mitchell Plain

The Mississippian Plateau in Kentucky, and its counterpart in Indiana, the Mitchell Plain, are often described as some of the world's best examples of karst topography. Translated into simple language, this means a lot of sink holes and underground drainage. In many ways the terrain of these upland plateaus is similar to that of the Outer Blue Grass and the Muscatatuck Regional Slope, but

Siderite pestle from a site in the Falls area

a trip through the upland plateau will show that there are few creeks and streams. This is because the limestone bedrock has been dissolved and most of the drainage is underground. Portion of rivers, like the Green River in Kentucky, flow underground and gigantic cave systems, such as Mammoth Cave, have been created. For prehistoric people in the Falls area the nearby Mississippian Plateau and Mitchell Plain provided a vital natural resource, a high quality chert for making chipped stone tools.

Natural Resources

Besides food resources, each of these geographical areas provided prehistoric populations with natural resources. It is immediately apparent in looking at chipped stone tools from prehistoric archaeological sites in the Falls area that they are made for a number of different cherts. (Chert is an impure form of flint.) These will range in color from

View of the Knobs in southern Bullitt County, Kentucky as seen from State Road 44

Isolated knob in southern Bullitt County, Kentucky

white to dark gray, and reds that range from crimson to pink. Some cherts are speckled with shades of brown and even hues of yellow and blue are present. Each of the physiographic provinces in the Falls area yielded a unique kind of chert and these give the archaeologist a clue to the extent that prehistoric people exploited these provinces.

Two of the common cherts that prehistoric people in the Falls area used can be found in the Knobs and Normal Upland. It is not known if the exact location of geological outcrops were known to Native Americans, but it would have been easy to obtain chert without knowing the source. Out-wash areas, gullies, and stream beds are often littered with chert and would have made it easy to collect. Two different kinds of chert can be found in the Knobs and Norman Upland and for convenience they have been called Type I and Type II. Type I chert is mottled, or variegated, with colors ranging from light pink to red, light tan to brown, and shades of white and gray. These colors will appear together in the same block of chert and grade into each other. Type II chert is characterized by small, colored dots called oolites. These are small pockets that have been formed around grains of sand. Like Type I chert, Type II chert occurs in a variety of colors that include browns, reds, yellows, and blues.

Type I chert found in the Knobs and Norman Upland

Type II chert found in the Knobs and Norman Upland

Type III Wyandotte chert found in the Mississippian Plateaus and the Mitchell Plain

Portions of the Mitchell Plain in Indiana, and the Mississippian Plateaus in Meade County, Kentucky, provided Native Americans with a chert of such a high quality that it might be called flint. The author has called this Type III chert and it ranges in color from light gray to almost black. Prehistoric people recognized the high quality of this chert and it was utilized by groups living far beyond the Falls area. Various names have been given to this chert, such as Wyandotte chert and Indiana Hornstone, but people in the Falls area have tagged it Harrison County chert after the enormous workshop sites that have been found in this Indiana county.

The Outer Bluegrass limestones also contained a chert that was utilized in prehistoric times. Of all the cherts found in the Falls area, this was probably utilized the least, It is white to grayish-white in color and contains small linear and circular fossils. Perhaps the main source of this chert in prehistoric times was the Falls of the Ohio River since these chert bearing limestones were exposed in this area. For convenience this is referred to as Type IV chert.

The last glacier left behind sizable quartz and granite pebbles on the flood plain of the Ohio River and at the Falls, and Native Americans found these ideal for making ground stone tools such as, axes, celts, pestles, and rolling pins. Water-worn chert pebbles were also utilized for making chipped and ground stone tools and the author has called these Type V chert. They are usually glossy in appearance with colors of pink, red, white, yellow, and brown. A water worn surface on an artifact is a clue that it was made from a pebble chert.

By observing the different kinds of cherts at a site, and the frequency with which they occur in different stratigraphic levels, it is possible to see a trend in how the different sources were utilized. Excavations conducted by the author showed that during Middle and Late Archaic times the chert sources closest to the site were the ones that were usually utilized. By Woodland times, knowledge of the high quality Wyandotte chert must have been wide-spread and people were willing to bypass nearby chert sources and make trips to Harrison County, Indiana, or Meade County, Kentucky, to get this material.

There are some natural resources in the Falls area that may have been utilized prehistorically, but their use has not been verified. Occasionally a projectile point will be found with traces of a dark substance adhering to the base. This material is called asphaltum, or bituminous sandstone, and it was used as

Type IV chert found in the Outer Bluegrass and at the Ohio River Falls

Type V pebble chert found on the flood plain of the Ohio River and the Ohio River Falls

an adhesive to secure the point to the shaft. The closest deposits of this material to the Falls area are about 45 miles to the west in Breckinridge County, Kentucky. Although this is the closest source, it does not necessarily mean that this was the one that was exploited.

Finally, what role did the buffalo play in prehistoric times? Early settlers discovered numerous buffalo traces in the Ohio Valley and many of these served as early pioneer roads. It appears that the buffalo entered this area relatively late and, to the author's knowledge, no bones have been found associated with Archaic, or Early or Middle Woodland sites. It was only Mississippian people, and perhaps after AD 1000, who were able to add them to their diet.

The purpose of this chapter has been to expose the reader to the geographic diversity of the Falls of the Ohio River region. It was this diversity that yielded a great variety of food and natural resources and permitted prehistoric people to thrive in great numbers. The author has even suggested that game and plant resources were available in such abundance that, prior to plant domestication, groups in the Falls area may have been able to have semi-permanent settlements.

The J. Graham Brown Site

While a few sites in the Falls area have produced projectile points from the Paleo-Indian period, the first people to come to the area in any number were Early Archaic hunters and gatherers. They arrived around 8,000 B.C. and settled in temporary camps along the tributaries of the Ohio River. In the mid 1950s the author discovered one of these camps in a cornfield on the J. Graham Brown farm. It was located east of Breckinridge Lane and just north of the Middle Fork of Beargrass Creek. Today this is the main parking lot of the Baptist East Hospital.

The site covered several acres and evidence of prehistoric occupation consisted of chipped stone artifacts, hammerstones, waste flakes from making stone tools, and fire-cracked rock from fire pits. This assemblage of tools suggests that a variety of activities were taking place. Projectile points reflect hunting, scrapers suggest the cleaning and processing of hides, and hammerstones indicate that tools were being manufactured on the site. These early inhabitants were probably highly nomadic and may have returned to the site seasonally to hunt game, fish in Beargrass

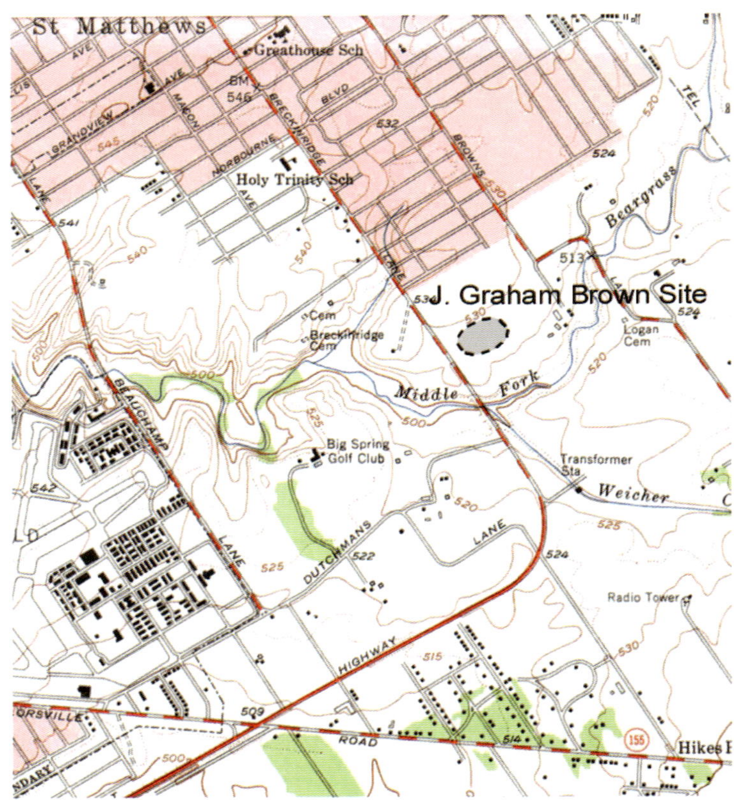

USGS 1951 Topographic Map Showing the J. Graham Brown Site. At the time of this map the Watterson Expressway had not been constructed east of Breckinridge Lane.

Early Archaic projectile points (Kirk type) from the J. Graham Brown site

Creek, and gather wild plant foods. Evidence that allows us to infer that these were Early Archaic people is in the shape of the projectile points that they left behind. The most frequent type found on the site is called a Kirk point, and cross dating with other sites where there has been radiocarbon dating, places them in the 8000 to 6000 B.C. time range. It is interesting to note that all of the Kirk points are from a chert that is found in the Knobs and called Type I in the last chapter. This reflects that these Early Archaic hunters were familiar with the chert resources in the Knobs. The presence of Knob chert waste flakes on the surface of the site, and several large preforms made from this material show that artifact manufacturing was being done onsite. A preform is a partially worked piece of chert that requires minimal flaking to be converted into a finished artifact. It is assumed that these were made at, or near, the source of the material since it would be easier, and more efficient, to transport partially finished artifacts than blocks of raw chert.

The Kirk points were not the only Archaic period projectile points from the site. In addition to other Early Archaic point types, some dating from the Middle and Late Archaic periods were also found. This reinforces the assumption that this was a favorable location for a site and inland streams like the

Preforms from the J. Graham Brown site

Middle Fork of Beargrass Creek were important prehistoric highways .

It should be noted that not all Archaic projectile points were made with cherts from the Knobs, and even during Early Archaic times the high quality, gray Wyandotte chert sources from Harrison County, Indiana, or Meade County, Kentucky, were being utilized. Since the Early Archaic spans at least 2,000 years, it is not known if finding both Knobs and Wyandotte cherts is indicative of two different groups of people, or if these two chert sources were utilized at different times.

Early, Middle and Late Archaic Projectile Points from the J. Graham Brown Site

The variety of tools, other than projectile points, recovered from the site suggests that this was not a short term camp, but that people lived here for some duration. Most likely this was a seasonal site that was occupied for several months by four or five families. They were engaged in making artifacts, processing hides for things such as clothing and bedding, and the drills found on the site tell us that they were drilling something. There is no direct evidence of what this was, but on Archaic sites where

There are no known wooden tools from the Archaic period, but it is logical to assume that they were present. Perhaps holes were drilled in wood for artifacts whose function we will never know.

There is scant evidence of people on the J. Graham Brown site after 1,500 to 1,000 B.C., and we must jump ahead about 2,500 years before people return to the site in any numbers. Five triangular arrow points show that people were on the site during Late Woodland times. By this time the subsistence base of Native Americans was based on domesticated plants, particularly maize and squash, and the settlement pattern was one of settled village life. From the small number of Late Woodland artifacts found on the site, it is unlikely that this was a village. It appears more likely to be a candidate for a temporary site used by hunters. Although domesticated plants were grown, game was still an important part of the diet.

Drill fragments from the
J. Graham Brown site

there is bone preservation, needles have been found that were fashioned from deer bone. These have a hole drilled in them which must have been made with a stone tool. The needle was probably an important tool in converting hides into useful items, and we can only speculate that it was used in conjunction with plant and animal fibers to make bags and nets. Occasionally archaeologists find flat stones that have been shaped and polished that have a hole drilled in them. It is assumed that these are pendants. From an Archaic site in the Falls area, the author has seen a bird bone with holes drilled in it so it resembled a whistle.

Arrow points fragments from
the J. Graham Brown site

One other Late Woodland artifact was found on the site that was not expected. It was a small fragment of pottery with impressions of cords on the surface. This was a common surface treatment found on Late Woodland pottery. It is speculated that if this were a hunting party, a pottery vessel might have been carried in a hide or fiber basket along with other provisions. It was only after the pottery from another Late Woodland site (the Muddy Fork site, also discussed in a later chapter) was analyzed, that the importance of this single pottery sherd was known. The reader will be left in suspense, and will discover in the discussion of Muddy Fork site pottery what makes this single sherd so important.

Late Woodland pottery sherd
from the J. Graham Brown site

Looking north from the Kaden Tower at the Baptist Hospital East and the location of the J. Graham Brown site (October, 2006)

The Clarksville Site

The Clarksville site was located in Clark County, Indiana, adjacent to the Falls of the Ohio River, and across from Louisville, Kentucky. Its exact boundaries are not known, but it was probably the largest site in the region. Today the site no longer exists, not as a result of commercial or residential development, but because of natural causes. The spring flooding of the Ohio River cuts into the bank of the river and, when the flood waters are high, large portions of the bank are washed away. It was during these times that relic collectors would hunt for artifacts and probably thousands were found. No doubt many times this many were washed away by the river.

Although the Clarksville site had been known for decades, it received little attention from professional archaeologists. Only twice have controlled excavations been done, once in the 1930s when E.Y. Guernsey conducted excavations for the Indiana Historical Society, and in the summers of 1969 and 1970 when the author directed more extensive excavations. The discussion of the Clarksville site will be based almost entirely on the latter work.

The 1969 and 1970 excavations were conducted by laying out units that measured five-by-five feet and digging them in three inch levels. This would slice the deposits

Erosional bank of the Ohio River at the Clarksville site - 1969

A three-foot layer of midden exposed
in the river bank at the Clarksville site

A total of fifteen units were excavated during the two summers of work and the average depth of deposits was three feet (12 three-inch levels). Charred hickory nuts were collected from some of the levels and submitted for radiocarbon tests. The sample from level 6 dated 2920 B.C. and two samples from level 9 (one from Unit D and the other from Unit E) both dated 3210 B.C.

The projectile points found at the site were mostly heavy stemmed forms like the McWhinney and Rowlett types, and a lesser number of notched points like Matanza Side Notched (also called Salt River Side Notched). There was a higher frequency of stemmed points in levels 1 through 5 and more corner and side notched in levels 6 through 12. There appeared to be a gradual transition from one style to another. Some stemmed points were found in the lowest levels and side notched points occurred in the upper levels.

in thin sections and, by relative dating, make cultural material older as the levels got deeper. In order to recover smaller artifacts and non-artifacts, all dirt was screened through a one-quarter-inch mesh.

The cultural deposits at the Clarksville site consisted of artifacts such as chipped and ground stone tools, and non-artifacts that represented food remains. These included deer and small animal bone, fish bone, freshwater mussels and snails and charred nut fragments. In addition, there were thousands of chert waste flakes from tool-making, and fire-cracked rocks that probably lined fire pits. This complex of artifacts and non-artifacts were mixed with a dark brown soil. Archaeologists call this matrix "midden," which is a fancy name for "garbage."

The beginning of the 1969 excavations

Clarksville Site Artifact Inventory
Excavated Units A - O

Chipped Stone Artifacts

Projectile Points	62
Drills	23
Hafted Scrapers	10
Bifacial End Scrapers	5
Knives or Small Preforms	11
Large Preforms	23
Gravers	5
Biface Fragments	90
Unifacial End Scrapers	11
Unifacial Side Scrapers	50
Unifacial Notched Scrapers	13
Worked/Utilized Flakes	37
Total	**340**

Ground Stone Artifacts

Axe Fragments	2
Pestle Fragments	6
Netsinkers	2
Hammerstones	28
Pitted stones	3
Whetstones	2
Flat-Rounded Disks	3
Unidentified Fragments	26
Total	**72**

Bone and Antler Artifacts

Needles	10
Awls (mammal bone)	31
Awls (bird bone)	10
Needle or Awl Fragments	201
Fishhooks	46
Bird Bone Beads	4
Drilled Canines	2
Atlatl Hook Fragments	2
Polished Fish Spines	11
Turtle Shell Bowl ?	1
Drilled Skunk Jaw	1
Cut-Polished Fragments	81
Antler Projectile Points	12
Antler Flakers	1
Cut-Polished Antler Tines	28
Total	**441**

Shell Artifacts

Bead	1

SUMMARY

Chipped Stone Artifacts	340
Ground Stone Artifacts	72
Bone and Antler Artifacts	441
Shell Artifacts	1
TOTAL ARTIFACTS	854

Projectile points from the Clarksville site

In Chapter 1, the reason for using the term "projectile point" was explained, but it is now time to elaborate on this. The term "arrow" or "arrowhead" implies that it was propelled with a bow. Actually the bow does not arrive in the Eastern United States until Late Woodland times around A.D. 500 or 600. Therefore archaeologists use the descriptive term "projectile point" to describe the pointed, notched and stemmed tools that were used before the bow was introduced. Projectile points were attached to the end of a shaft and either thrown by hand, or launched with a spear thrower called an "atlatl" (pronounced at-lat-el). If this is difficult to pronounce, it is because it is an Aztec word. The concept behind the atlatl is that the longer a person's arm, the more force that can be generated in throwing something. For example, with a fishing pole, it is possible to cast further with a six-foot pole than one three feet long. An atlatl is a hand-held wooden shaft that artificially lengthens one's arm. The rear shaft of the spear rests on the back of the atlatl and the spear is balanced by curling the index finger around the shaft.

The reason for describing the atlatl is to introduce an artifact originally called a "bannerstone" and referred to as an "altatl weight" by archaeologists. The atlatl was composed of a wooden shaft with a bone or antler handle at one end, a stone in the middle, and a bone or antler hook at the other end. The central stone is the atlatl weight, and a hole was drilled through it so it could be attached to the atlatl shaft. The hook helped balance the rear of the spear shaft against the end of the atlatl. This three-component concept of the atlatl is based on excavations of the Indian Knoll site on the Green River in Kentucky where burial goods included atlatl weights associated with antler hooks and handles.

The most interesting feature of an atlatl weight is the hole that was drilled through the center of the stone. In many cases, atlatl weights were made from river pebbles that were quartz. Yes, using stone age technology it would be difficult to drill a quarter-inch diameter hole through two to

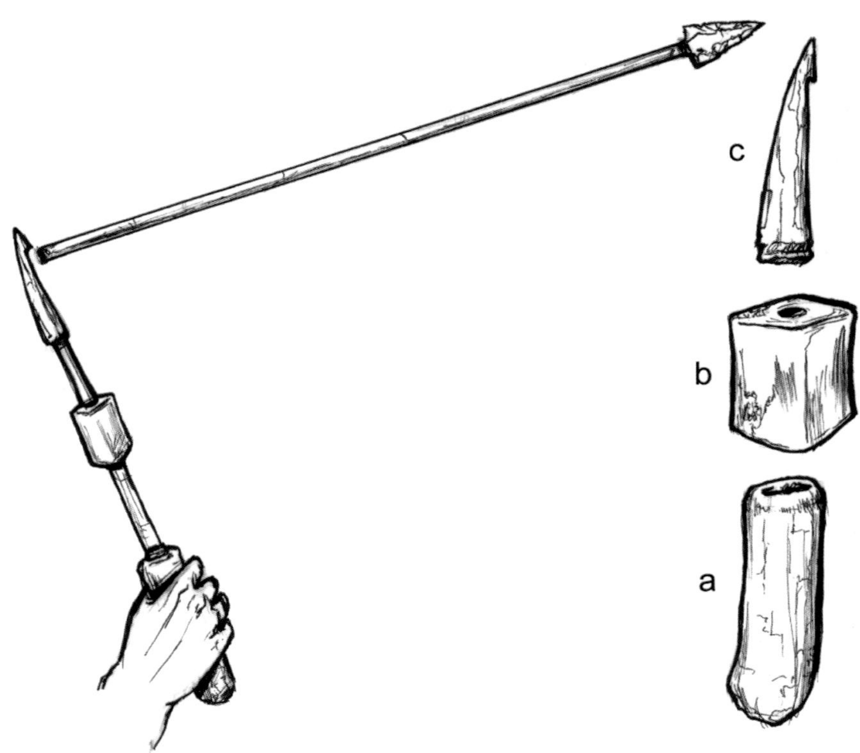

The atlatl and its components (a) handle, (b) atlatl weight, (c) hook
(Drawing by Leigh Bader)

Atlatl weight and deer bone hook from the Clarksville site (James J. Matthews collection)

three inches of quartz. The technique that appears to have been employed was to use a hollow reed as the drill and something like fine quartz sand as the abrasive. The weight was finished by finely grinding and polishing the surface. Unfinished atlatl weights have been found with the hole only partially drilled. These will often have a stone cylinder projecting up from the bottom of the hole. This is the uncut portion of the stone that went up the hollow part of the reed.

Although a large number of atlatl weights have been found, their function is still debated. Finding these drilled stones associated with antler hooks and handles in burials is powerful evidence that they served as a weight on the atlatl. However, it can be argued on logical grounds that an artifact that takes hundreds of hours to make did not function as a tool, but had some symbolic meaning. This is why these finely made and polished drilled stone artifacts were initially called bannerstones. It was reasoned that they were mounted on the end of a shaft and served as a symbol of authority. It has recently been suggested that since these artifacts were made in a variety of shapes, they were perhaps clan symbols. Based on the high number of these drilled stones found associated with burials, maybe their purpose was to serve as mortuary items and they were tied to the belief system of the people.

It should be noted that the atlatl is used by the Australian aborigines and was historically used by many different Native Americans tribes in South America. In all these instances a weight is not used. Regardless of how this debate is concluded, a number of atlatl weights have been found on Archaic sites in the Falls area.

In the first chapter the five things that the archaeologist observes were listed. Of particular interest at the Clarksville site was the non-artifact data. The 1969 and 1970 excavations attempted to recover as much data as possible and as the dirt was being screened everything was saved. This was a time-consuming process because even the smallest pieces of chert and bone were collected. As a result, over 30,000 chert waste flakes were collected. These were the by-products of making chipped stone tools and they revealed the process that was followed in making these tools. The waste material that is created in chipping a tool from a block of chert can be contrasted to getting a piece of finished lumber from a tree. Before the tree goes to the mill the bark and branches must be removed. The first step in making a tool is to remove the exterior from the stone. This cortex is the bark of the chert and it is not

suitable for making tools. There are also large angular pieces of chert removed in this process. After the bark and branches are removed from the tree it is rough cut into lumber and the scrap material is smaller. As a block of chert is fashioned into a tool, smaller flakes are produced. The final stage at the lumber mill is to plane the wood and this results in fine wood chips and saw dust. The final flaking of a tool produces very small flakes as it is shaped into its final form. From the kind of wood debris found at a lumber yard it is possible to tell what operations took place. If there are very few scraps of bark residue it would indicate that the initial processing of the log had been done somewhere else. This same logic is used by archaeologists to tell if the initial flaking was

Drills from the Clarksville site

Knives from the Clarksville site

done at the source of the chert, or if it was done back at the settlement. At the Clarksville site the analysis of the 25,000-plus waste flakes indicated that 42% of them were from the first stages of making a tool. The remainder represented the subsequent steps that end in a finished tool. This means that the people at Clarksville were bringing whole chunks of chert back to the site from the source and making tools there.

In the chapter on Physical Setting it was mentioned that five different kinds of chert can be found in the Falls region, so the question is, where were the people at Clarksville getting their chert? Each of the waste flakes were sorted into one of these five chert types and 64% were from Type I and II cherts that are found in the Kentucky and Indiana Knobs. These were easy for the people at Clarksville to obtain since the Knobs are about four miles away. The next most commonly used chert was the whitish Chert Type IV which can be found in limestones that outcrop at the Falls. Pebble cherts, which can also be found in gravels at the Falls, accounted for 9% of the waste flakes. The only reason the reader has been subjected to these percentages is to point out that all but 4% percent of the chert used at the Clarksville site was from nearby sources. It seems logical that people would uses resources that were locally available, but it is the dark gray Wyandotte chert (Type III) from the Mitchell Plain that is the highest grade chert and the easiest to work. To get to the source of Wyandotte chert the people at the Clarksville site would have had to travel 25 to 30 miles. Tools and waste flakes made of this material do occur at the Clarksville site.   The fact that it was not utilized to a greater extent probably reflects nothing more than local cherts were suitable for meeting their tool making requirements. During the Early Woodland period this changes and people bypass local cherts in favor of Wyandotte chert.

While most people are intrigued by the artifacts that Native Americans made, it is the non-artifacts that excite the archaeologist because they allow a glimpse into the culture of prehistoric people. One reason that every scrap of bone was collected during the 1969 and 1970 excavations was to get data on what the people at the Clarksville site ate. Fortunately our excavations were in a prehistoric dump and soil conditions were favorable for bone preservation.   As the dirt was being screened it was apparent the white-tailed deer, small mammals, fish, bird, and freshwater mussels and snails were part of the

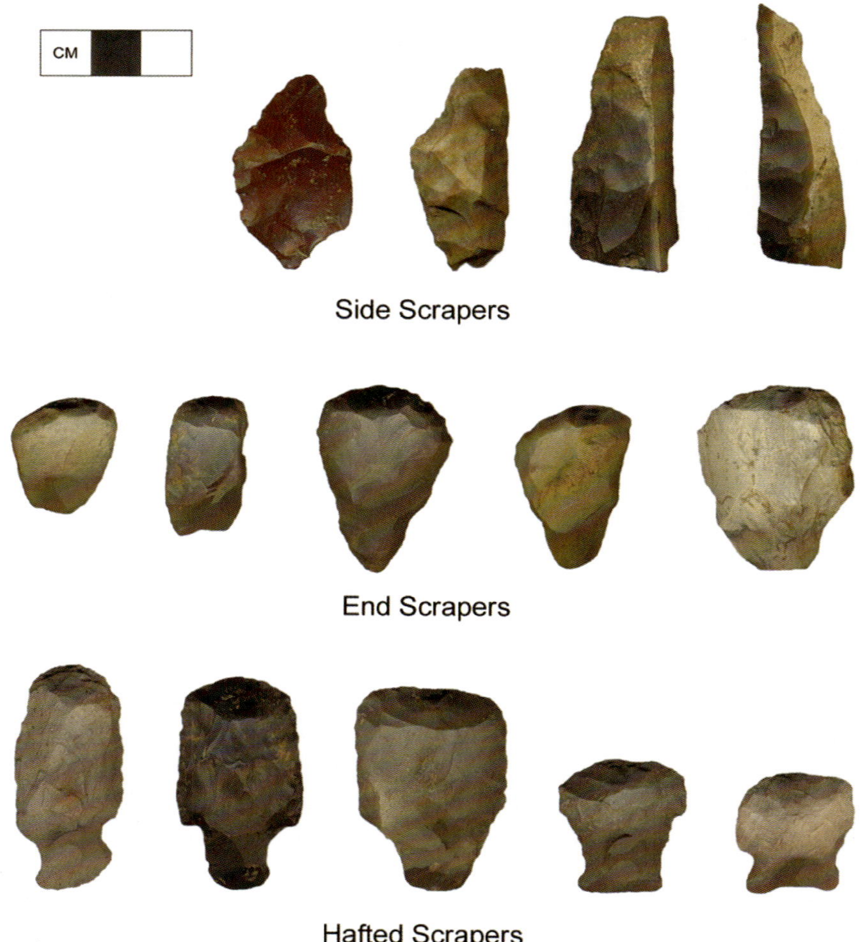

Three types of scrapers from the Clarksville site

Aerial photograph showing the location of the 1969 excavations (Photograph by Billy Davis)

diet. However, archaeologists are not content just to generate a laundry list of items in the diet. What we would like to know is the relative importance of these foods to the people who lived at the Clarksville site.

In Chapter I, Archaeology 101 for the public, the five things the archaeologist observes were listed. The last item on that list was "Quantities". Applying quantities in this case means counting bones, and this is how we can reconstruct how important certain foods were in the diet. Actually doing this is a time consuming process. For each three-inch level there was a separate bag and everything had to be washed. Next it was sorted into artifacts, chert waste flakes, bone, antler, and shell. Each piece of bone that was large enough to be identified was separated into classes such as deer, small mammal, turtle, bird, and fish. The deer bone was then identified by kind, for example upper leg (tibia), and then if it was

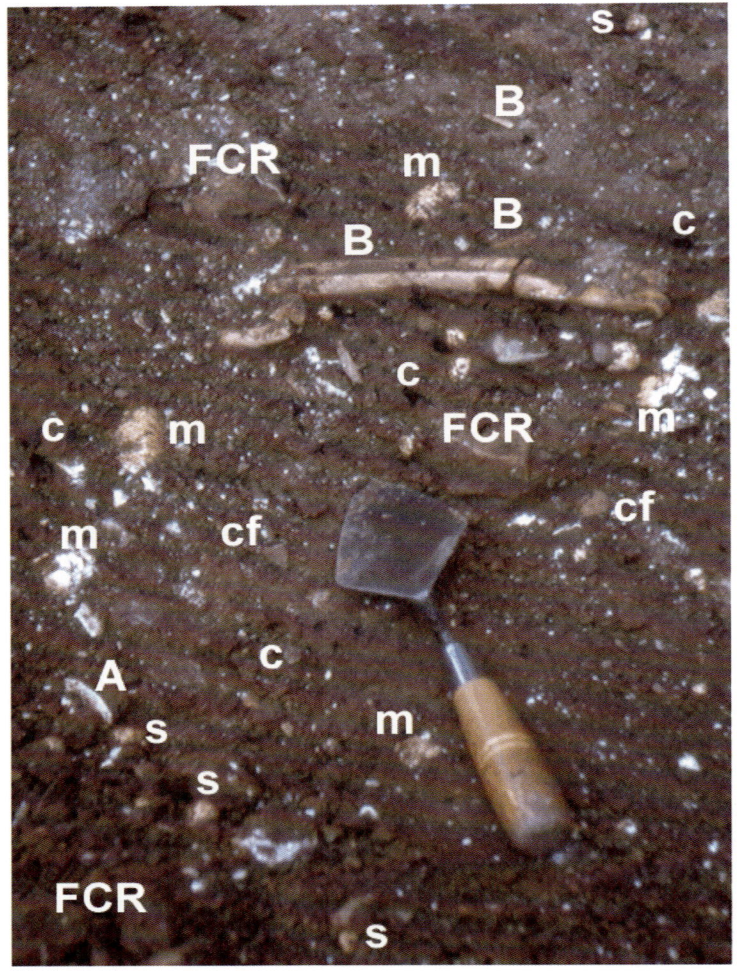

A - chipped stone artifact

B - animal bone

FCR - fire-cracked rock

cf - chert waste flake

c - charcoal

m - mussel shell

s - freshwater snail

Typical floor of a unit at the Clarksville site

the left or right. After this has been done the number of bones in each category was counted and the largest number in one category represents the minimum number of deer that are represented.

The eight units excavated in 1969 contained 3,378 deer bones. When the bones were classified and sorted into groups there were 111 bones of one of the toes on the left foot. This means that the excavations recovered the remains of at least 111 deer. If the average weight of a dressed deer is 125 pounds, then this represents 13,875 pounds of venison. It is interesting that there were only a few bones from small game such as racoons, opossum, and rabbit. These apparently played a small role in the diet. The excavations also recovered some turkey bone, but none from migratory birds such as ducks and geese. Besides food animals, a few dog bones were recovered. We should not forget that the domestication of our cold-nosed friend goes back thousands of years.

Since the Clarksville site was located adjacent to the Falls of the Ohio River, it is not surprising that it was a source of food. The two items utilized the most were fish and freshwater mussels. It is interesting that only one land animal, deer, was dominantly exploited for food, and similarly only one fish was extensively utilized. This fish was the freshwater drum. A distinguishing feature of the freshwater drum is its ear bone, called an otolith. These are a dense oval bone and they were well preserved at the Clarksville site. This bone was used to determine the minimum number of individuals recovered in the 1969 excavations. A total of 809 left otoliths were identified meaning that at least this many freshwater drum were represented in the bones that were recovered.

Fortunately, in the case of freshwater drum fish it was possible to take the analysis one step further. A study was done by Arthur Witt Jr. where the length and weight of freshwater drum were measured, and the otoliths were extracted and their length and weight recorded. Witt was able to derive an equation that gave the relationship of these variables. The length of each of the 809 left otoliths from the 1969 excavations was measured and the equation used to determine their live length and weight. The results showed that the average freshwater drum caught by the people at the Clarksville site was fourteen inches long and weighed about one pound and three ounces. The largest otolith corresponded to a fish that was almost three feet long and weighed 27 pounds, and the total weight of all 809 freshwater drum was 1,660 pounds.

There is good evidence of how the people at the Clarksville site were catching freshwater drum. A total of 46 fish hooks, made from deer bone, were found in the excavations as well as small, rounded river pebbles (the size of a golf ball or smaller) with a shallow groove pecked around them. Archaeologists have traditionally called these rounded stones "net sinkers" and it is assumed that they were used in conjunction with net fishing. The freshwater drum is a bottom feeding fish, like catfish, and in order to make fishing with a hook effective a line sinker must be used.   Using logical evidence, it is concluded that these grooved river pebbles

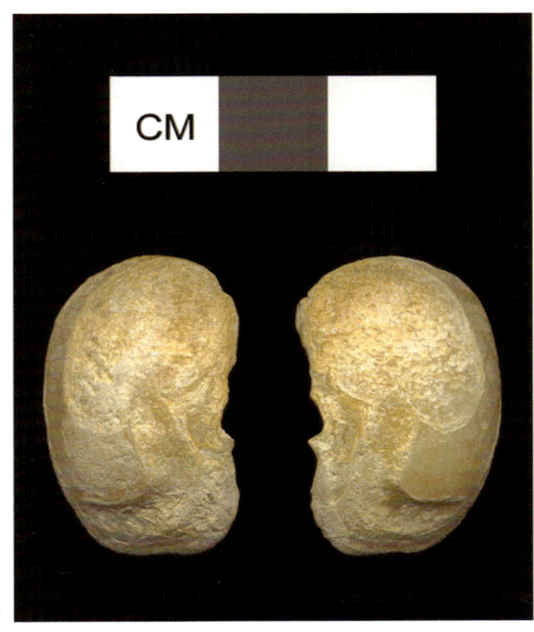

Freshwater drum fish otoliths

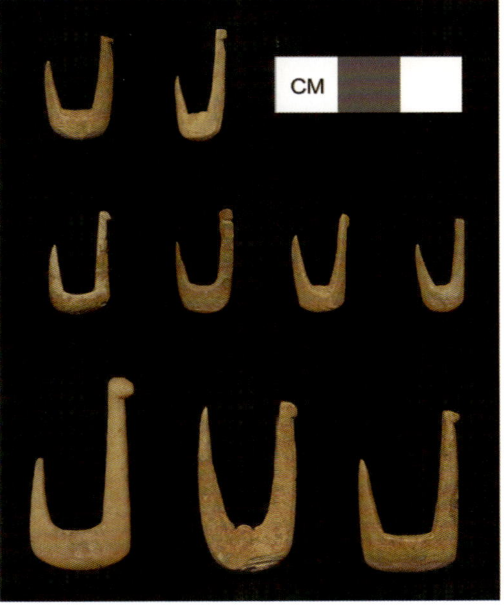

Fishhooks from the Clarksville site

Linesinkers from the Clarksville site

at the Clarksville site were used as line sinkers to sink the hook so bottom-feeding fish could be caught.

Another food that the Falls provided was freshwater mussels. These were present in large quantities, but since they were very brittle, the majority broke as soon as they were recovered. It was therefore not possible to get an accurate count or determine their density in the midden.   Mussel shells are common in Late Archaic sites that are adjacent to rivers and streams so we know that they were an integral part of the diet.

What was not expected was the large number of freshwater snails. They did not occur in concentrations, or layers, as might be expected if they had been washed onto the site during a flood, but were evenly distributed throughout the deposits. They were so prolific that they were all saved from Unit C so an estimate could be made for all the units. Five different kinds of freshwater snails were

Freshwater mussels and snails from the Clarksville site

identified and the number from Unit C was 24,715. This was an average of 2,060 snails per three-inch level or 296,640 for the 144 levels that were excavated in 1969. Given the other foods in the diet it is puzzling why a low yield food like snails would be so popular. A cache of freshwater snails was found at the Indian Knoll site in Ohio County, Kentucky, so they were not unique to the Clarksville site. The answer to why they were present in such numbers at the Clarksville site may be very simple, people enjoyed them.

Direct evidence of plant foods at the Clarksville site was limited to charred nut shells fragments. They were sprinkled through the midden like pepper on a steak and served as the material that was dated by radiocarbon analysis. These dates turned out to be 2,920 B.C. and 3,210 B.C. Since the shells were so fragmentary no count was taken, but hickory and walnut dominated. Six ground stone pestles fragments were recovered from the excavations and many more have been found on the surface by collectors. Large stone rolling pins, similar in shape to our modern rolling pin, and nutting stones have also been found on the site. A nutting stone is a rock with a flat surface that contains hemispherical depressions. It is speculated that nuts were placed in these depressions and cracked. There is, of course, no proof of this, but it seems logical to infer that their function was to process some kind of plant food.

1970 excavations at the Clarksville site. The river has since eroded this area away.

Pestles

Rolling pin

Nutstones

Food processing tools from the Clarksville site

This is perhaps a good place to remind the reader that archaeologists use two main approaches in classifying a tool. One is to use a functional name, such as "spear" or "nutstone", and the other is to use a descriptive name like "pointed bifacially flaked tool" or "stone with hemispherical depressions." The use of functional names is of course a guess, but they can be highly accurate, as in the case of pestles. These tools have been used for thousands of years and have remained rather consistent in shape over time. Other artifacts, as we discovered with "netsinkers," may have been used in other ways.

The knowledge of ceramic making did not exist during Archaic times and it is difficult for us today to envision cooking without pots and pans. The people at the Clarksville site did have containers and the skull cap of a deer and the shell of a turtle were found that showed signs that they had been modified. Perhaps they were used as cups. We can speculate that most of their containers were probably made from wood and hides. There was some evidence of how food was cooked and one of the most frequent items recovered in the excavations were rocks that had been altered by fire. Archaeologists call these fire-cracked rock and a photograph of an excellent example is shown in Chapter 1 in the section on Glossary of Archaeological Terms. In order to gain an understanding of the amount of fire-cracked rock at the Clarksville site, it was saved from Unit H and weighed. Unit H (dimensions of five-by-five feet) was excavated to a depth of three feet (12 three-inch layers) and it contained 1,765 pounds of fire-cracked rock. This is about 147

One of the fire-cracked rock piles at the Clarksville site

pounds per three-inch layer. If this average is applied to all 144 three-inch levels that were excavated at this site a little over 10½ tons of fire-cracked rock was present.

In order to explore some of the ways food was prepared, a kind of logical evidence called "Ethnographic Analogy" will be used. An ethnography is the description of the culture of a people. In this case we want to research ethnographies of hunters and gatherers to see how they prepared food. This can be used as an analogy of how cooking might have been done at the Clarksville site. We discover that roasting on a spit over an open fire and smoking (particularly fish)are common ways food is prepared.

Two other cooking methods could account for the large number of fire-cracked rock at the Clarksville site. One is steaming food, and even today this is a popular way of cooking mussels. Freshwater mussels could have been placed on heated rocks and then quenched with water. This would not only steam cook them but would account for why the rocks were fractured. The other method of preparing food could have been by baking. A pit would be lined with heated rocks, the food placed on the rocks, and them completely covered with more heated rocks. The pit would then be filled with dirt, thus creating an oven. By controlling the number of heated rocks in the pit, the temperature of the oven could be regulated to cook several one pound fish, or five pounds of venison.

Another artifact from the Clarksville site that was probably related to cooking was about two hundred fired earthen balls (ranging in size from about a golf ball to a tennis ball). They were hand-molded into several shapes and have been called "cooking balls." What is fascinating about these artifacts is that there are few prehistoric archaeological sites in the Ohio River Valley that have produced these objects, but similar looking artifacts have been found by the hundreds of thousands at the Poverty Point site in northeastern Louisiana. It seems

Fired clay objects from the Clarksville and Poverty Point sites

logical to infer that these earthen objects were a kind of prehistoric charcoal briquette and were used the same way as rocks in cooking.

The intriguing question is, "How did these Poverty Point-looking objects get to the Clarksville site?" It is assumed that they were not independently invented so we are left with several options to explain their presence. They could have been (1) brought directly to the Clarksville site by people from the Poverty Point site who were exploring the Ohio River, (2) traded from group to group from Poverty Point to the Clarksville site (besides Poverty Point, these objects have been found at sites in the lower Mississippi River drainage), or (3) they were obtained by people from the Clarksville site who explored the lower Mississippi River area. At the present time, there is no good evidence for selecting one of these options over the other, so their presence at the Falls is still a mystery.

Besides being a source of food, deer, small mammal, fish and shell also provided the residents of the Clarksville site with another important commodity - material for making artifacts. There was excellent bone preservation at the Clarksville site and all bone was saved and carefully examined. As a result, it was discovered how tools were made since all the various stages of the manufacturing process were present. The long bones of deer (front and rear legs) seems to have been preferred.   The first step was to use a hammerstone to remove the ends of the bone. This was done by battering a depression around the end of the bone and then breaking it off. In making a needle or awl, a chert knife was used to cut the bone lengthwise

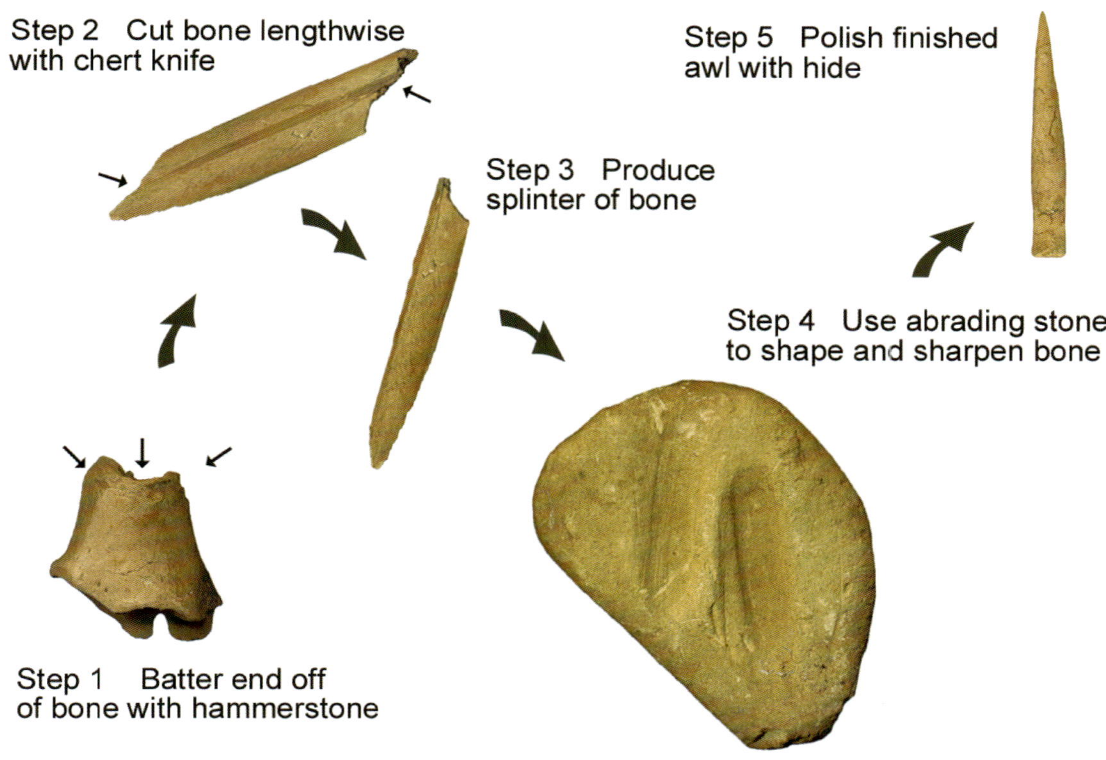

The steps involved in making an awl from deer bone

Deer bone awls from the Clarksville site

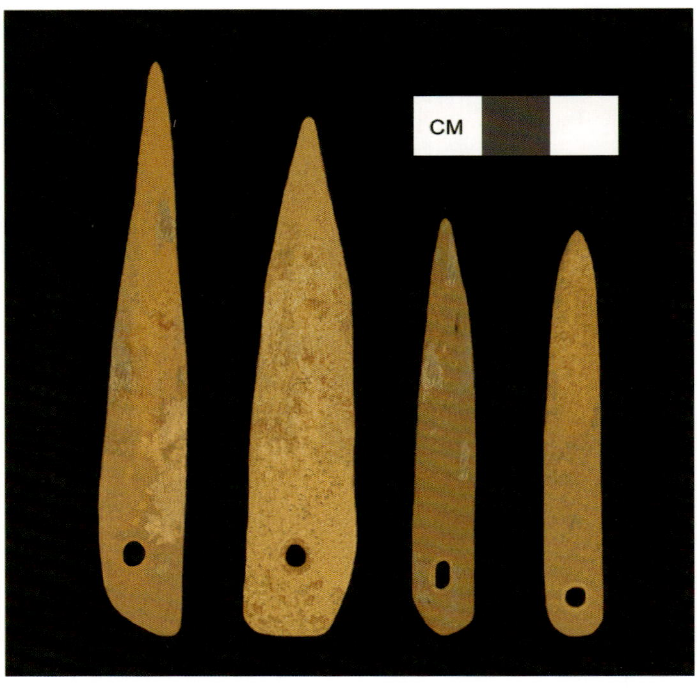

Deer bone needles from the Clarksville site

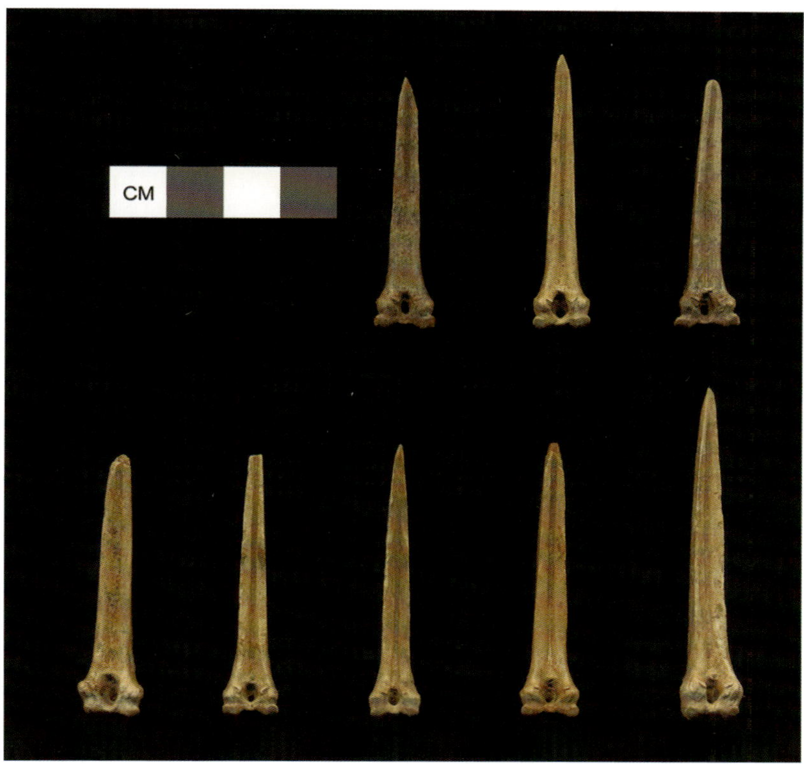

Freshwater drumfish spines used as awls and/or needles

into strips and do the preliminary shaping of the tool. A stone, such as sandstone, was next used as a file to give the tool its final shape and it was then probably buffed and polished with a hide.

The spines of freshwater drum fish needed almost no modifications to be adapted as awls and needles. It is usually difficult to determine if a spine was used in this way without a microscopic examination. When bone is used repeatedly to puncture hides, or any soft material, it becomes polished and produces a sheen. Some of the fish spines recovered in the excavations displayed these characteristics. This same procedure was used to determine if a chert tool had been used as a knife. The ridges of the tool will become rounded and polished if it is used to butcher meat or cut wood. The knives (shown earlier in this chapter) were each examined microscopically and determined to have rounded and polished ridges.

The tip (tines) of deer antler were removed by cutting around the antler and snapping off the pointed end. The end was then used as an awl, or was modified so it could be attached to the end of a shaft and used as a spear point.

While we usually associate prehistoric hunters and gathers as having a "stone age" technology, there were more bone artifacts recovered in the 1969 and 1970 excavations than ones made from stone. In the same way that flaking a spear produced a lot of chert waste flakes, making a bone tool created many scrap fragments. Many of these fragments show that the common way to reduce a bone

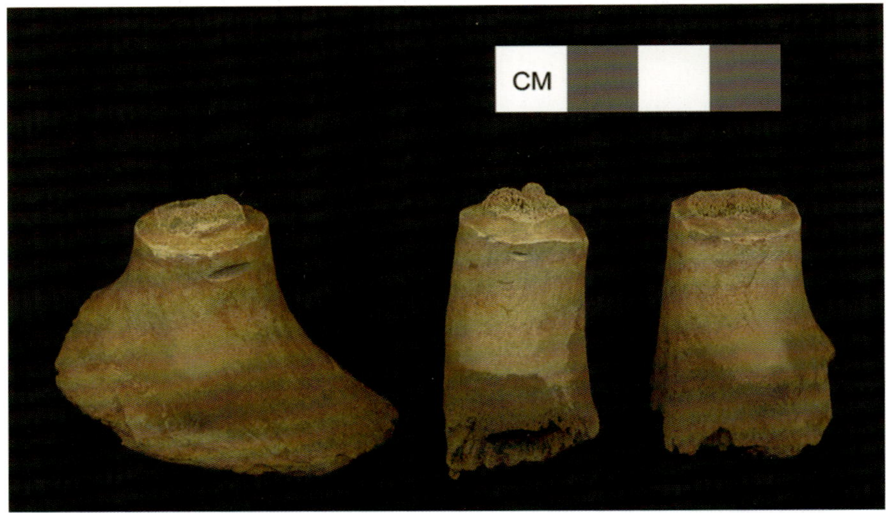

Cut-snapped antler residues from the Clarksville site

Cut-snapped deer long bone fragments from the Clarksville site

into pieces was to partially cut through the bone and then snap off the unwanted portion. This appears to have been the first step in making a bone fishhook.

So far the discussion of artifacts has focused on those that related to hunting, fishing, plant processing, and domestic activities. By emphasizing these tools we can get a distorted view of life at the Clarksville site. There was an aesthetic side to the culture that is reflected in some of the artifacts. There was time in the daily lives of these people to devote to making items of personal adornment. Beads were made in a number of ways. Holes were drilled in the canine teeth of dogs or racoons, and bird bone was cut into sections and polished. Freshwater mussel shell was carved into disks and a hole drilled in the center. Pendants were made by drilling a hole in a flat, polished stone and one was found where a hole had been drilled in the

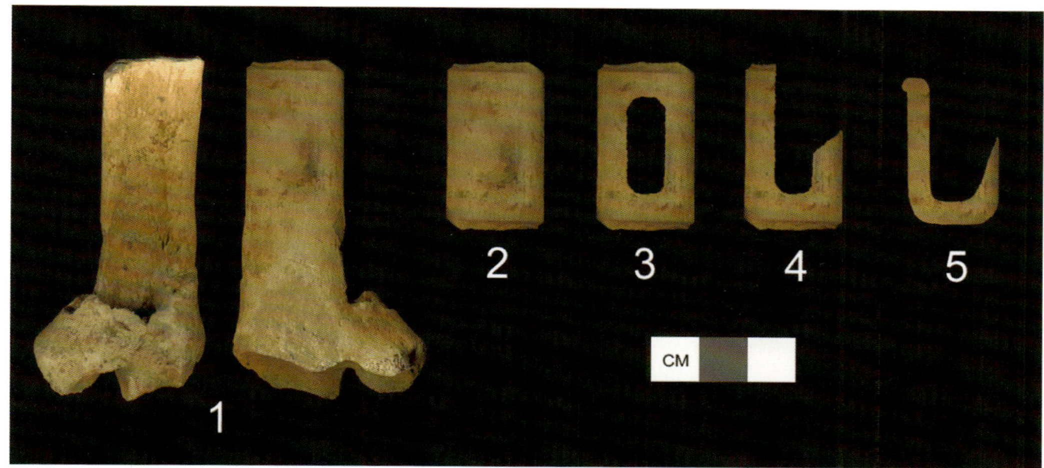

The steps involved in making a fishhook

jaw bone (mandible) of a skunk. Other artifacts in collections from the Clarksville site include long bone pins (speculated to be hair pins), elaborately shaped needles and awls, and a section of bird bone with a series of drilled holes was found on the site. Could this have been part of a flute or whistle?

It is obvious from some of the stone and bone artifacts found at the Clarksville site that some of these people were superb craftsmen or artisans. One place these artistic talents were exhibited was in decorating utilitarian bone tools such as awls and needles. This was done in one of two ways, either carving a row of notches or engraving designs into the bone. The designs were usually comprised of straight lines, zig-zags, cross hatching, and various forms of rectangular patterns. These designs were not confined to the Clarksville site, but have been found on bone tools at other Late Archaic sites in the Falls area.

We can only speculate on other places where decoration and design were used. It

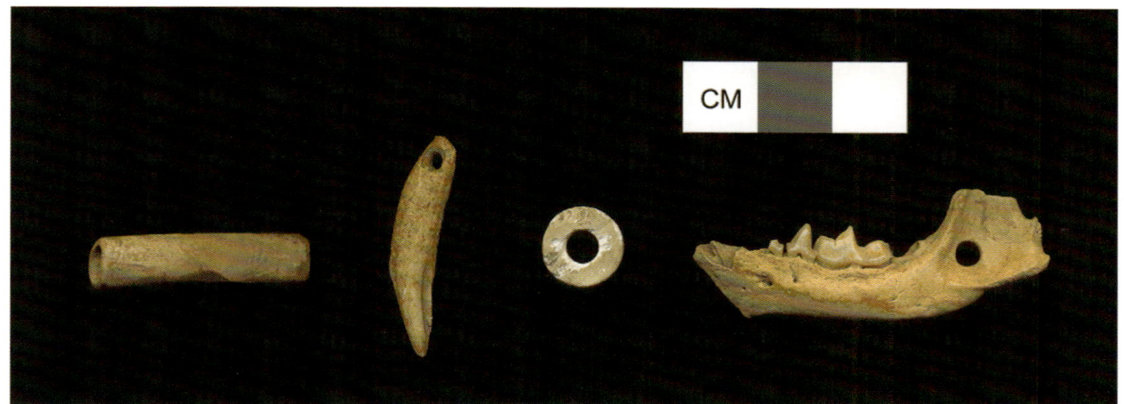

Items of personal adornment from the Clarksville site. From left to right, bird bone bead, canine tooth bead, mussel shell bead, drilled skunk jaw pendant

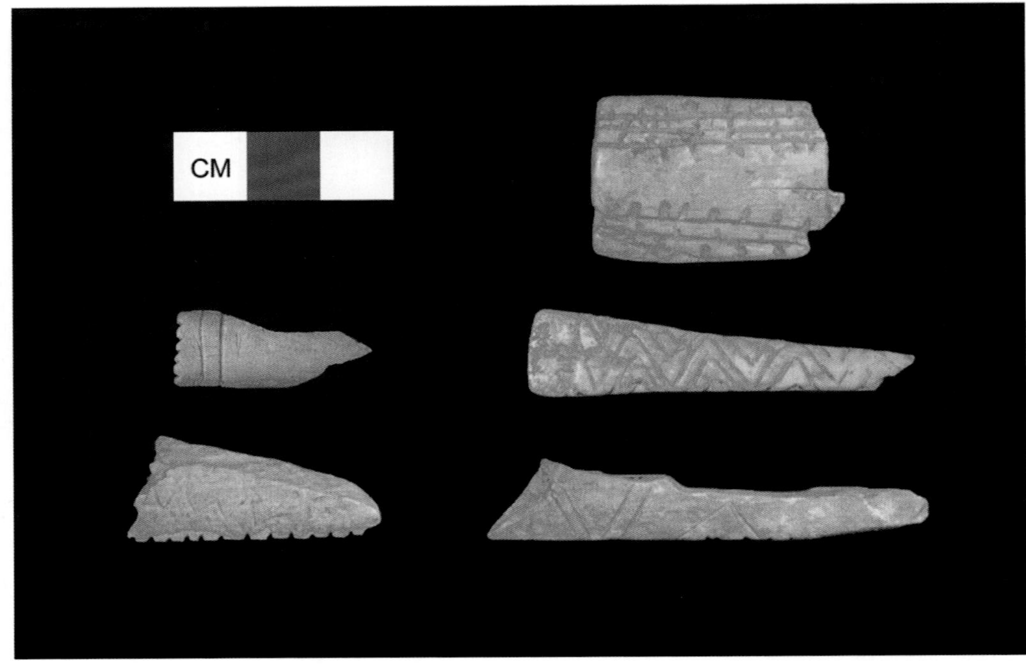

Examples of notched and engraved bone from the Clarksville site
(This photograph has been converted to black and white to accent the engraving)

seems logical to assume that the designs we see on bone artifacts were also applied to wooden ones. On a speculative level it is possible that colored ochers (which naturally occur in the Falls area) were used to decorate clothing or even the body. Yes, cosmetics go back this far in time.

It is difficult to estimate the area that the Clarksville site may at one time have covered since it has now been washed away. From what is known about the distribution of artifacts on the surface, it covered at least a third of a mile of waterfront. Archaeologists usually think of an archaeological site as a closed area where people lived and carried out their daily activities. While this is a logical way to think of a site, the conditions around the Falls of the Ohio River may have offered other settlement possibilities. This was an area of extremes, with fast-flowing rapids and calm eddies. Winter floods could produce high water while small pools were created in the summer when the river was low. Some places were no doubt better for gathering fresh-water mussels than others, and there were probably particular spots where fish could be easily caught. Since these kinds of places were scattered along the Falls, the settlement may have reflected this. Instead of congregating in groups, one or two extended families might have camped along the river adjacent to one of these ideal locations.

Perhaps a visitor arriving at the Falls in the evening would not see a cluster of campfires, but would be greeted with a constellation of flickering lights all along the bank of the river, and maybe even on some of the small islands that were just off shore. Although somewhat dispersed, these groups would still consider themselves part of the same community and the Falls would be their neighborhood.

1969 aerial photograph of the Ohio River looking toward the McAlpine Locks
and Dam, and the city of Louisville, Kentucky   (Photograph by Billy Davis)

Lone Hill and other Wet Woods Sites

Next to the Clarksville site, the Lone Hill site in Jefferson County, Kentucky, may have been the most intensely inhabited place in the Falls region during Late Archaic times. It covered a vast area that is now part of Louisville's Standiford Field International Airport. The site derived its name from a small, loaf-shaped, solitary hill that was probably an erosional remnant of a knob. It was introduced to archaeologists in the 1950s when the Ford Motor Company took dirt from around the hill and used it as fill where an assembly plant was to be built on Fern Valley Road. At that time there were no professional archaeologists working in the Louisville area and it was left to collectors to salvage information about the site.

In the early 1950s the closest runway at Standiford Field was over a mile from Lone Hill, but since then multiple expansions of the airport have destroyed the site. Fortunately, with these expansions, professional archaeologists were given an opportunity to conduct excavations and learn more about the prehistory of the area. The predominant occupation of the Lone Hill site took place during Late Archaic times, although there are artifacts representing the Early and Middle Archaic, as well as from the Woodland period.

What is interesting about the Lone Hill site is that it is located in the Kentucky Scottsburg Lowland, and adjacent to an area that early settlers called the "Wet Woods."

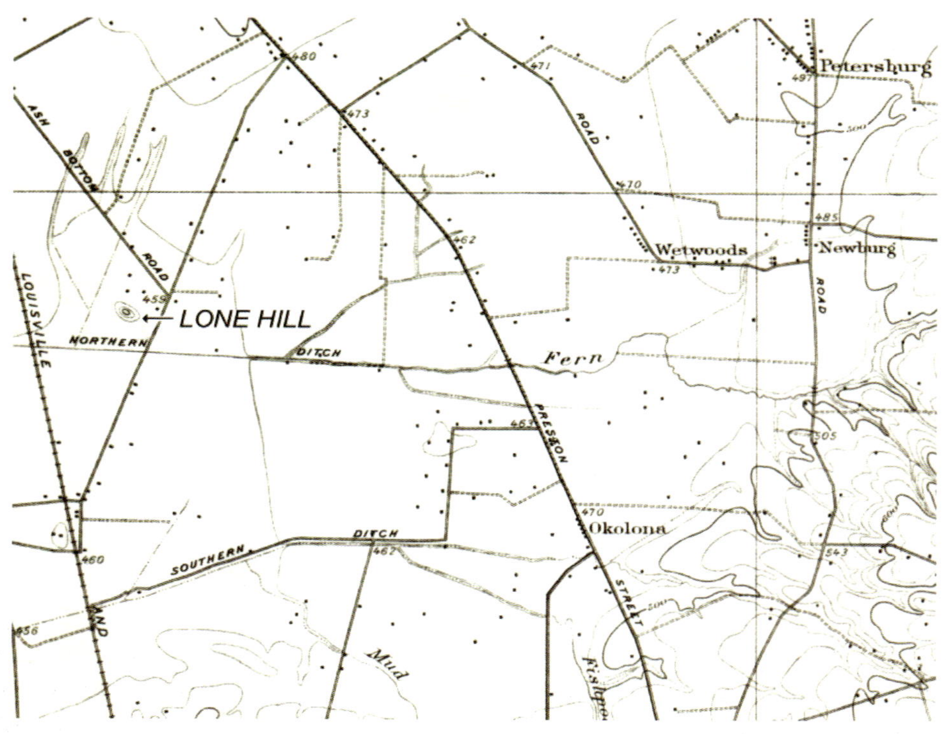

1907 U.S.G.S topographic map showing the location of Lone Hill

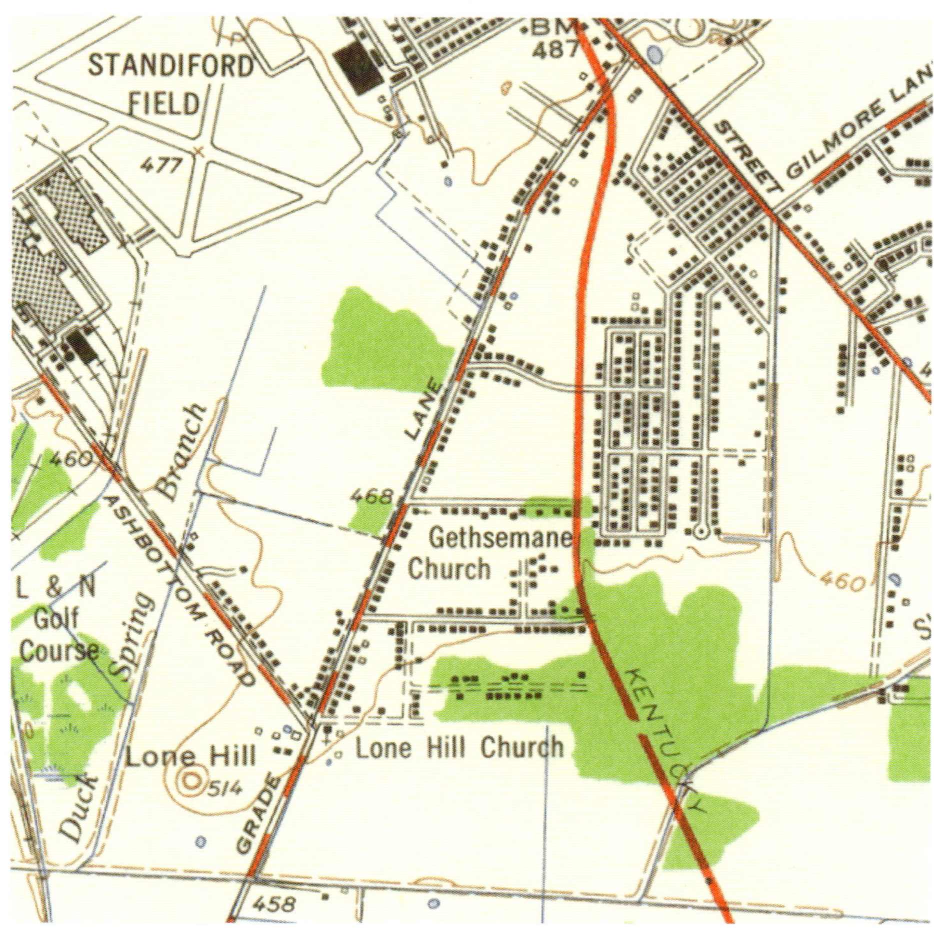

1951 U.S.G.S. topographic map showing the location of Lone Hill
with respect to Louisville's Standiford Field

This name was even given to a small community located west of Newburg Road and east of Preston Street, and is shown on the 1907 United States Geological Survey topographic map. The reason that the wetland exists is because it is underlaid with shale, not limestone like the surrounding area. While limestone bedrock can be eroded and dissolved by slightly acidic water, shale cannot and it acts like an underground dam as water seeps through the soil. Streams, like Fern Creek and its tributaries, run through the Scottsburg Lowland and these, along with natural springs such as Duck Springs and Blue Spring, helped in creating the wetland environment. Two areas with a slightly higher elevation created islands within the wetland and these were known as Big Island and Lost Island.

The presence of this low wetland area is not something that recently formed. Since the shale bedrock has been present for hundreds of millions of years, streams that flowed though the area during Archaic times probably created the same kind of Wet Woods

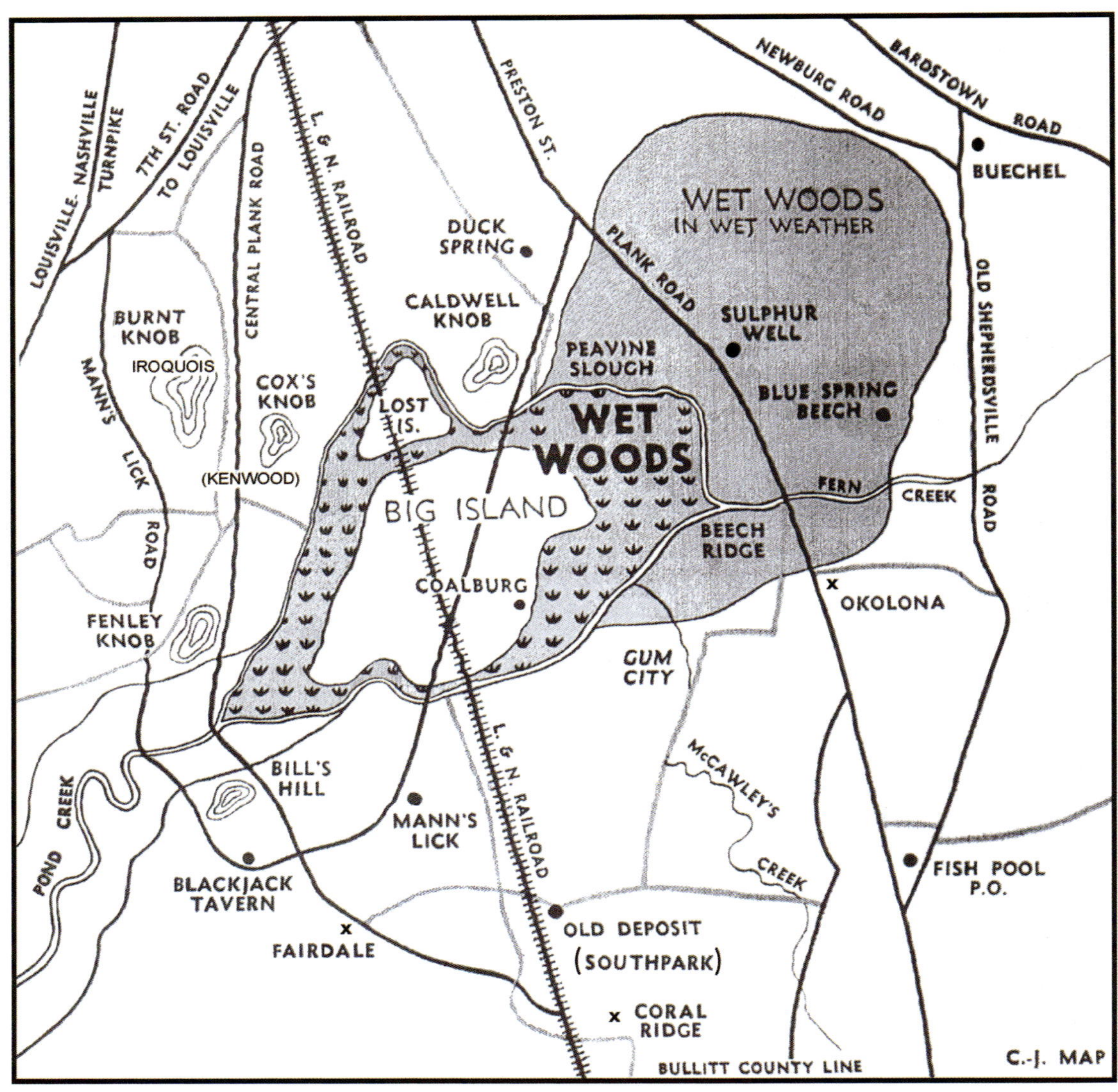

A reconstruction of the Wet Woods area based on early historical records. Lone Hill is called Caldwell Knob. Burnt Knob is now part of Iroquois Park and Cox's Knob is today called Kenwood Hill. This map appeared in the June 8, 1941, Louisville *Courier-Journal.* (© *The Courier-Journal*)

environment that the early settlers encountered. To rectify the drainage problems in this area, in the early part of the 20th century two drainage canals, called the Northern Ditch and the Southern Ditch, were excavated. Fern Creek flows into the Northern Ditch while several creeks drain into the Southern Ditch. These eventually merge and empty into Pond Creek, which is a tributary of the Salt River. Both the Northern and Southern Ditch are shown on the 1907 U.S.G.S. topographic map.

The Southern Ditch today as it drains the Scottsburg Lowland

This rather detailed discussion of the Wet Woods has been given since the Lone Hill site was perhaps the largest prehistoric site ever found in Jefferson County, and it was located adjacent to this wetland area. In fact, several other large prehistoric sites have also been found bordering what was the Wet Woods. We do not know exactly what attracted prehistoric people to this area. From historic accounts we know that the Wet Woods teemed with fish that entered the lowland when the water was high and were trapped in pools when the water receded. It must have been easy to catch fish since a 1941 *Courier-Journal* article refers to an historic account of fishing with a pitchfork. In Chapter 2 on Physical Setting, the study by Charles Gunn is cited as referring to the Kentucky Scottsburg Lowlands as having plant life that is unique to this part of the state. Perhaps plants are the key that drew prehistoric people to this area. Maybe they were an important supplement to their diet, or it was the plants that drew animals to the area and made hunting as easy as fishing. Whatever attracted prehistoric people to the Lone Hill site, their culture, as reflected in their artifacts, appears to be typical of the Late Archaic in the Falls region. They cannot be considered some specialized "Swamp Archaic," or an offshoot from mainstream Late Archaic. Some of their artifacts show a high degree of craftsmanship and the axe shown on the cover and title page of this book was found at the Lone Hill site.

It is impossible to know how many prehistoric artifacts have been found at the Lone Hill site, but a safe estimate would

A photograph of Lone Hill looking northwest from Grade Lane
(© *The Courier-Journal*)

probably be 5,000. Projectile points are the key artifact for placing the site into a temporal framework. Two common forms found at the Lone Hill site were a long, narrow point with a stemmed base, and a small, side-notched point. The stemmed variety is a common form found on Late Archaic sites and is called a McWhinney Heavy Stemmed type (or a Rowlett point which is similar, if not the same). The side-notched points have been classified as two types called Matanzas Side Notched and Brewerton Eared-Notched. The author found a number of these points at a site in southwestern Jefferson County, about fifteen miles from Lone Hill, and lumped the two types into one called Salt River Side Notched. This is mentioned since this type is referred to in the literature. Salt River Side Notched points were found associated with deposits that had radiocarbon dates (recalibrated) from 4,500 B.C. to 2,500 B.C. (The term "recalibrated" means that the original dates have been recalculated based on newer data about radioactive carbon.) These dates can be used to fix a time period for similar projectile points found at the Lone Hill site. This technique of applying dates of artifacts from one site to similar artifacts at another site is called "cross-dating."

Archaeologists assume that culture is patterned and that when a projectile point was made it followed some standards in the mind of the person making it. While this might be

Salt River Side Notched projectile points from the Lone Hill site
(Projectile points on the bottom row and hafted scrapers on the top row)

a valid assumption, it is probably equally valid to assume that there were slight variations on this standard. Native Americans did not stamp out artifacts like modern machines stamp out identical parts. For example, if the goal was to make a point with side notches there may have been an "ideal" place in the mind of the maker as to where the notches should be located on the blade, and on their size and depth. However, the configuration of the base may not have been that important and could be concave, convex, or straight. While there are Late Archaic projectile points that seem to share a number of attributes, it seems that the majority do not. This has led to putting them into broad categories like "Late Archaic Stemmed" where there is considerable variability in blade shape, basal configuration, and length. This was certainly true of the projectile points from the Lone Hill site and there seems to be an endless variation of shapes based on the common theme of a stemmed projectile point. The book by Noel Justice (cited in the reference section) makes an excellent attempt to sort out the variations in Late Archaic projectile point types.

One of the things that the archaeologist notices about the artifact assemblage from Late Archaic sites is that the people recycled their artifacts when they broke. This was probably true of earlier and later groups as well, but it seems to be particularly pronounced during Late Archaic times. Perhaps it was the effort that was required to walk to the sources of chert and to carry heavy loads back to the site that encouraged recycling. Broken projectile points were not always discarded but the basal end was saved and the broken part reworked into a hafted scraper. (If the reader has forgotten what a hafted scraper is, it is defined in the glossary

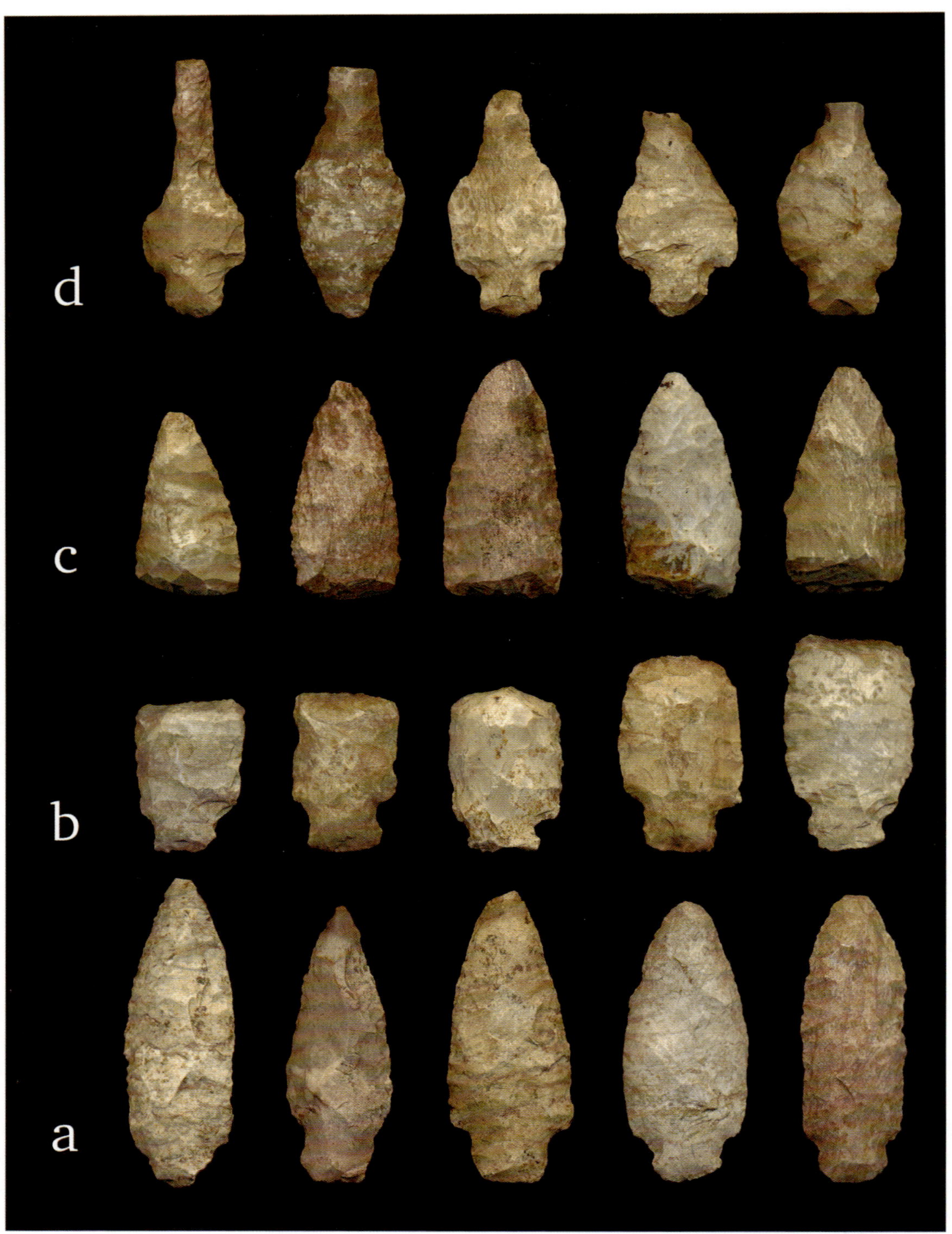

Chipped stone artifacts from the Lone Hill site. Row a - projectile points; Row b, hafted scrapers; Row c, scrapers, probably made from the tips of projectile points; Row d, drills

Variation in Late Archaic stemmed projectile points from the Lone Hill site
(most of these can be classified as McWhinney or Rowlett, which is similar)

of terms at the end of Chapter 1). There are examples from the Lone Hill site of the tips (probably from broken projectile points) being saved and the broken end reworked into a scraping tool. There are examples of drills that look like they were made from a projectile point, and waste flakes derived from chipping artifacts show signs that they were used as scraping and cutting tools. When cores were too small to produce flakes many were used as hammerstomes.

The reader may have noticed that the artifacts that have been pictured are not always symmetrical and many lack fine secondary flaking. This does not mean that the people who made them lacked the ability to produce finely made artifacts. As anthropologists, archaeologists realize that a culture must be evaluated from within the framework of the people in that culture. This is called "cultural relativity." What may seem crude to us was perhaps functional for them. Projectile points were flaked to the degree that they could achieve their purpose. Anyone who has ever grown tomatoes knows that they must be staked. The stakes that are used are always rough cut and it is not necessary that they be straight. The artifacts that have been pictured were efficient for hunting, or

Preforms of Type I chert from the Lone Hill site

to be used for cutting and scraping. To have spent more time flaking and shaping them would be like sanding and painting tomato stakes.

One of the things that is immediately apparent in looking at a collection of chipped stone artifacts from the Lone Hill site is that most of them are made from cherts that in Chapter 2 were called Type I and Type II cherts (see page 22). These cherts are found in the Norman Upland of Indiana and the Kentucky Knobs. While some artifacts are made from the high grade Type III Wyandotte chert, these are mostly artifacts that date from either the Early Archaic or Early Woodland. The Scottsburg Lowland in Kentucky is bordered to the south and southwest by the Knobs, and like the Late Archaic people at the Clarksville site, the Lone Hillers were utilizing the cherts that were the closest to their settlement. It would have been a six-mile hike to the chert sources that the author has found in the Knobs southwest of Fairdale, or two miles closer to the South Park hills just north of the Bullitt County line. A large number of preforms and partially worked chunks of Type I and II cherts were found on the Lone Hill site. It seems reasonable to assume that chert was being brought to the site partially worked. It is easier and more efficient to remove the unusable exterior (called the cortex) of the chert at the source and carry only the usable material back to the site.

There may be some readers who have artifact collections from the Falls area and are interested in chert sources. They may wonder why Type I chert has not been called Muldraugh Chert since it is found in the Muldraugh geological formation. There are two reasons for this. For this book, the purpose of knowing chert types is to tell us what geographical regions were being exploited in prehistoric times. We have discovered that the people at the Lone Hill site were obtaining the majority of their cherts from the Knobs. For our purposes, knowing the exact places in the Knobs is not important.

The second reason is that the author does not want to give the reader the impression that Native Americans were familiar with the Muldraugh formation, knew where it outcropped, and went there to obtain chert. Perhaps they did. While Native Americans probably got some cherts by going to the formations, they did not have to do this to get Muldraugh chert. The author has walked the Kentucky and Indiana Knobs on many occasions looking for chert and has found that some stream beds and erosional gullies are full of Type I and II cherts. It has no doubt eroded from the formation into these places and could be collected without going to the source. Type II chert can be found with Type I and may be from the same source.

There is one other property of Type I and II cherts that should be mentioned. Archaeologists have discovered that in some cases Native Americans heated chert before it was worked. Experiments have shown that this enhances the properties of the material and makes it easier to flake. It is also known that some cherts take on pink to red colors when they are heat treated. The reader may have noticed that many of the chipped stone artifacts that are pictured from the Lone Hill site have these colors. Some of these artifacts may have been flaked from chert heat treated by Native Americans, but it is unlikely that they all were. In the case of Type I and II cherts, they naturally occur in pink to red colors. Perhaps these colors are the product of heating that occurred in the geological formations when they were formed.

Naturally occurring red examples of Type I chert (collected by the author from a stream bed in the Jefferson County Knobs, three miles west of Fairdale, Kentucky)

Nut stone from the Lone Hill site

Other stone artifacts found at the Lone Hill site include chipped stone drills and a variety of different kinds of scraping and cutting tools. A number of axes and pestles, both whole and broken, were collected and it is estimated that a hundred were found. Perhaps the most spectacular axe, in terms of size and workmanship, from the Falls area was found at Lone Hill. This axe is pictured on the cover and title page of this book. One of the materials used to make pestles was a low grade iron ore (hematite or siderite) that can be found in the Knobs. There are at least two known 19th century iron furnaces in Bullitt County that were utilizing these ores. Nut stones were also recovered from the site reflecting that their function at the Clarksville site was being duplicated at Lone Hill.

From the bone found at the Lone Hill site, white-tailed deer was the main source of food. While the presence of fishhooks and line sinkers provided evidence of fishing at the Clarksville site, to the author's knowledge, neither of these artifacts were found at the Lone Hill site. This does not mean that fish were not part of the diet. The conditions that created the Wet Woods (shale bedrock) were present during Archaic times and it is logical to assume that the later historic accounts of fish being trapped in pools also occurred then. If early settlers could use a pitchfork to catch fish, then we can make an ethnographic analogy and assume there is a good possibility that spear fishing was done by prehistoric people at the Lone Hill site. To review, an ethnography is a description of the culture of a people, and an ethnographic analogy is a kind of logical evidence where the cultural practices of one group are seen as a possible practice of another group, if conditions are the same. Here the common condition is the Wet Woods environment and fish trapped in shallow pools.

A number of whole and broken bannerstones were found at the Lone Hill site. Whether these served as weights on atlatls, or had some symbolic significance, it was something that was as important to the people

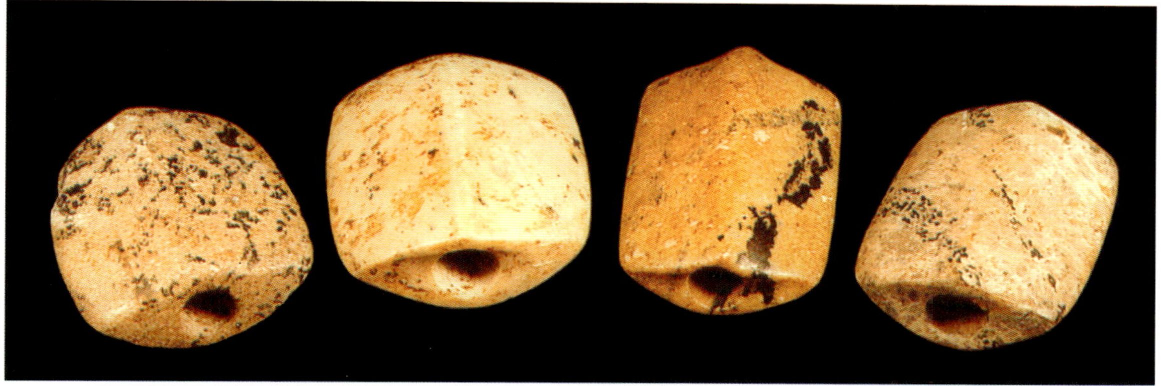

Bannerstones/atlatl weights from the Lone Hill site (photograph by Richard Burnett)

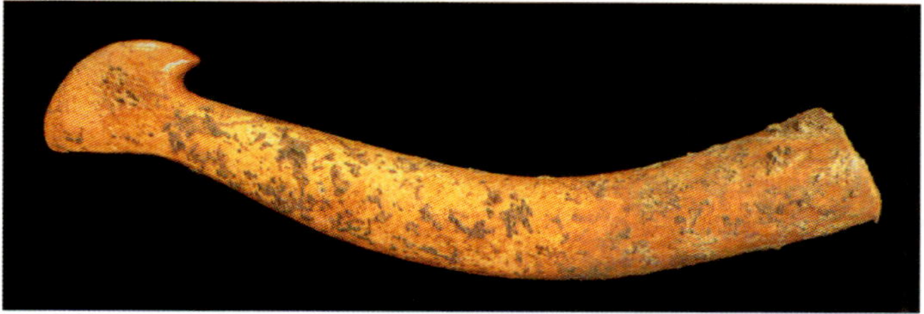

Atlatl hook from the Lone Hill site (Larry Swan collection, photograph by Richard Burnett)

living in the Wet Woods as it was to the inhabitants of the Clarksville site on the Ohio River. The bannerstones pictured above average a little under three inches in length and three-quarters of an inch in maximum width.

So far there has been no mention of what kind of houses or shelters people had in Archaic times. During the Woodland period houses were often constructed around a series of vertical posts that were placed in excavated holes. When a post decayed it left a dark circular stain in the ground which the archaeologist calls a "postmold." From the outline of postmolds the size and shape of a house can be reconstructed. Postmolds are rare at Archaic sites and we can only speculate that Archaic houses were similar to those described in early accounts of Native Americans who were hunters and gatherers.

The frame of the house was probably small saplings that could be easily felled with a stone axe. The base of the poles were most likely secured in shallow holes, or a trench, and leaned against each other to form a "tepee" shape, or were bent to form a dome. A smoke hole was probably left in the center of the structure and the poles were covered with branches and thatch, or hides to make the structure waterproof. These were most likely small houses, easy to build, and were for a nuclear family (a couple and their children).

Lone Hill was not the only site adjacent to the Wet Woods and nearby were two other large Archaic sites. They were the KYANG and the Minors Lane sites. The presence of a number of large sites surrounding the Wet Woods is a testimony to the abundance of food resources that must have been present in this environmental niche.

Reconstruction of life in the Wet Woods
(Drawing by Leigh Bader)

The KYANG Site

The KYANG site was located on what at one time was the Kentucky Air National Guard portion of Standiford Field airport. In relation to the Lone Hill site, it was approximately one mile to the northeast. Although some local residents knew of the site, it was rediscovered during preparation work for the construction of several new facilities for the Air Guard. Dr. Joseph Granger, archaeologist at the University of Louisville, was asked to direct excavations of the area and he named the site KYANG, using the initials of the KentuckY Air National Guard. What makes the KYANG site important is that it is the only one in the Wet Woods area where extensive controlled excavations have been conducted. In addition, there are published reports on the findings, and the bone and antler artifacts from the site served as the basis of a Masters thesis at the University of Kentucky Department of Anthropology (see Bader in the Bibliography).

The site was located on a knoll near Duck Spring, one of several springs that existed in the Wet Woods. The springs are shown in the upper center of the *Courier-Journal* Wet Woods map and the run-off created a small creek called Duck Spring Branch, which can be seen on the 1951 U.S.G.S. topographic map. The springs were still in existence at the time of the excavations and is a testimony to their durability.

The major work at the site was done in the summer of 1973 when excavations were conducted and artifacts were collected from the surface. Some preliminary work was done in 1972, and final investigations were done

Duck Spring at the Standiford Field Airport in 1973. In the background is the International Harvester plant. (Photograph by Rolland Soule)

Excavations at the KYANG site in 1973 (Photograph by Rolland Soule)

in 1975. The excavations revealed two distinct stratigraphic layers, an upper brown soil zone resting on a dark brown layer that was sprinkled with freshwater mussel shells and snails. Projectile points from the upper level were predominantly Late Archaic stemmed types, such as McWhinney/Rowlet, while the Salt River Side Notched type was associated with the lower shell-bearing layer. This transition in the Late Archaic from small side notched points to larger stemmed ones has been observed by the author at other sites in the Falls area, but it seems to have been demonstrated first at the KYANG site.

One of the interesting finds at the KYANG site was the buried layer of dark soil that contained freshwater mussel shells. Approximately 8,000 shells were collected during the excavations, which covered 1,850 square feet. Profile drawings in the field notes, and photographs of the excavations, show a thin scattering of shell throughout Layer 2. This is in contrast to the Clarksville site, and other sites the author has excavated along the Ohio River, where mussel shells occur in dense compacted layers.

The archaeologist loves to find freshwater mussels and snails because these little critters are very particular about what kind of environment they will inhabit. Some species like shallow still water while others like deeper, fast flowing streams and rivers. Some species will live in cold waters while for others it has to be warm water. Mussels and snails are therefore excellent climate indicators and tell us what streams were like in prehistoric times. The author had an expert in molluscan fauna (someone who studies mussels and snails) examine a sample of freshwater mussels that were collected from the KYANG site. Twenty-one different species were represented, one of which is now extinct.

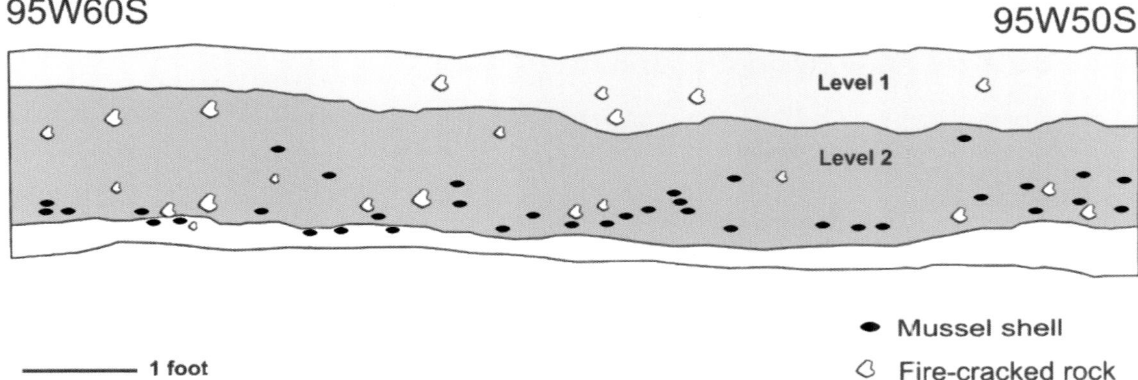

KYANG Site west wall profile, unit 95W60S
Profile drawing based on KYANG site field notes
(Drawing by Anne Bader)

All were identified as species that lived in medium to large rivers. The small streams and ponds that made up the Wet Woods would not have been a favorable habitat for these species of mussels.

We are now faced with the problem of trying to explain how freshwater mussels that come from a riverine environment could end up in the Wet Woods. The first thing to recognize is that freshwater mussels were probably a very small part of the diet at the KYANG site. The author was told by one of the crew members on the project that all mussel shell was collected, so 8,000 shells probably represent no more than 5,000 whole mussels. This many mussels could be consumed if ten people ate ten mussels a day for fifty days. We are, of course, just dealing with a sample of all mussel shells that are on the site. However, considering the size of the excavations, and the fact that the deposits the mussels were associated with represented hundreds of years, the number is still small.

There are several ways that river mussels could find their way into the Wet Woods. They could have been carried there by people living along the Ohio River during their seasonal movement into the Wet Woods. The Falls of the Ohio River is six miles to the north and is the closest source for these species of mussels. Perhaps people walked to the river and collected them. Several people leaving at dawn could hike to the river and be back in the Wet Woods by early afternoon. We can speculate that perhaps such a trip was made so some diversity could be added to the diet.

One advantage of excavating a site is that the dirt is screened and this allows a large quantity of material to be collected. Over 6,500 mammal, bird, and fish bone were retrieved from the site and from this we can get an idea of the diet of the KYANG people. As would be expected, white-tailed deer made up the bulk of the mammal bone assemblage. Given historic descriptions of the Wet Woods it is not surprising that fish were also important.   However,   when the author examined the collection, he discovered that almost all the fish bones were from freshwater drum, the same fish almost exclusively eaten by people at the Clarksville site.

We have logically concluded that fishing in the Wet Woods may have been with a spear and there is very little evidence at the

Dense mussel shell concentration at a site on the floodplain of the Ohio River, Floyd County, Indiana

Note the stratigraphy is similar to that found at the KYANG site with an upper brown soil layer over a lower dark brown soil that contains mussel shells (but at a much higher concentration).

KYANG site of line fishing. While bone fishhooks and stone line sinkers were common at the Clarksville site, only one fishhook, and two residual fragments, left over from making a fishhook, were found at the KYANG site. Not a single stone line sinker was found.

The KYANG collection is currently at the University of Louisville's archaeology curation facility and a description of each artifact, and where it was found, is recorded on a separate Artifact Record card which is on file. The author examined each of these cards and compiled an inventory of artifacts recovered from the excavated units. This was done so the KYANG site assemblage could be compared with the artifacts excavated at the Clarksville site. A total of 790 excavated artifacts are recorded from the KYANG site, of which 467 are bone and antler. This is 51% of the excavated artifacts, which is almost identical percentage (52%) of bone and antler

artifacts at the Clarksville site . It appears that we have misnamed the prehistoric past and it should be referred to as the Bone Age.

The most common bone and antler tools at both the KYANG and Clarksville site were awls and needles. It is assumed that these artifacts were used in conjunction with a range of domestic activities, such as making clothing, blankets, containers from skins, and perhaps weaving fiber nets and bags. It is apparent that these activities were equally important at both sites.

In addition to similar bone and antler tool inventories, the people at the KYANG site were also engraving bone artifacts, mostly awls and pins, with zig-zag, stair-step, and cross hatch designs. These are identical motifs to those found at the Clarksville and other Archaic sites along the Ohio River and its major tributaries.

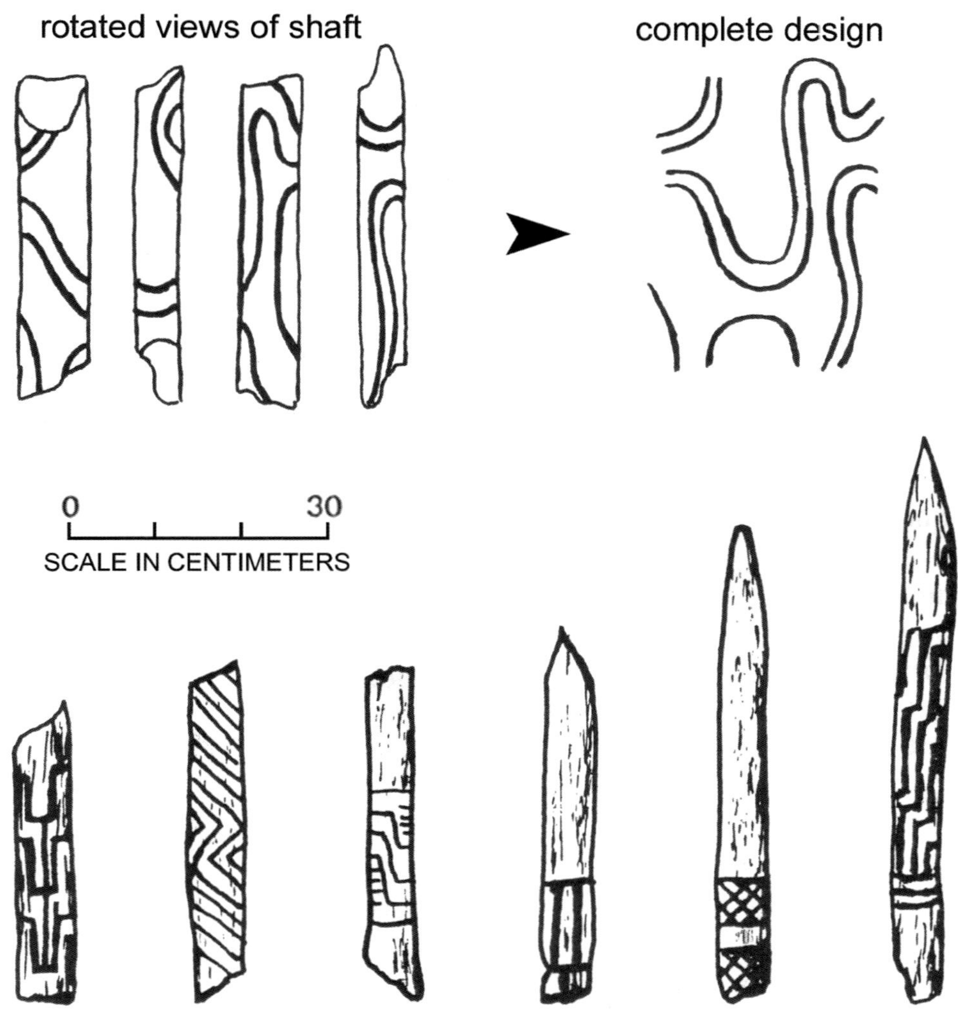

Engraved bone from the KYANG site
(Drawing by Anne Bader and used with her permission)

Besides stone and bone artifacts and food remains, the excavations also recovered approximately 150,000 chert waste flakes. These have not been analyzed, but the author visually examined about fifty boxes of flakes. The impression was that the majority of the chert was either coming from the Knobs (Chert Types I and II), or was the whitish Chert Type IV that can be found in the Outer Bluegrass. To the people at the KYANG site these would have been local cherts since the Outer Bluegrass boarders the Scottsburg Lowland to the north and east. The people at the KYANG site, like those at the Lone Hill site, were utilizing chert sources that were the closest to them.

KYANG Site Artifact Inventory from Excavations
(Based on artifact cards, University of Louisville, archaeology curation facility)

Chipped Stone (N = 311)		Bone and Antler (N= 467)	
projectile points	108	awls	167
drills	15	needles	48
hafted scrapers	13	pins	14
blanks and preforms	21	worked *	152
biface fragments	97	fishhooks/residues	3
scrapers (all kinds)	34	bone beads	2
choppers	1	drilled bone	2
utilized flakes	22	perforated bone	2
		antler flakers	30
Ground Stone N = 9)		all other	14
axe fragments	1	unidentified	33
abrader	1		
hammerstones	3	Shell (N=3)	
nutting stone	2	drilled	1
unidentified	2	unidentified	2

* includes pointed awl/needle/pin fragments and polished and worked fragments

Excavation units at the KYANG site in 1973 (Photograph by Rolland Soule)

A third large site in the vicinity of the Lone Hill and KYANG sites was just north of the South Park Hills and south of what is now the Southern Ditch. This site was known to amateur archaeologists as the Calhoun site, but it was introduced to the Louisville public on June 5, 1960. That morning the Louisville *Courier-Journal* ran an article with the headline, "Unearthed Indian Skeleton Believed To Be 5,000 Years Old". While grading a hill in preparation for the 700-home Minors Lane Heights subdivision, just west of Minors Lane, a bulldozer operator had uncovered a Native American grave. At that time there were no restrictions that would temporarily stop development activities, so it continued. It was therefore left to the amateur archaeologists to collect artifacts and salvage some information about the site. For some reason the old name "Calhoun site" was forgotten and the name became known as either the Minors Lane site, or the Shuck Lane site, which was a road just north of the proposed subdivision. It appears that the Minors Lane site is the name that has survived.

To the author's knowledge, a map of the site was never made, but from accounts of people who remember the area, artifacts were unearthed when heavy equipment leveled the hills west of Minors Lane. The location of the site can be estimated by following the higher contour lines on a U.S.G.S. map in the area where the subdivision was built.

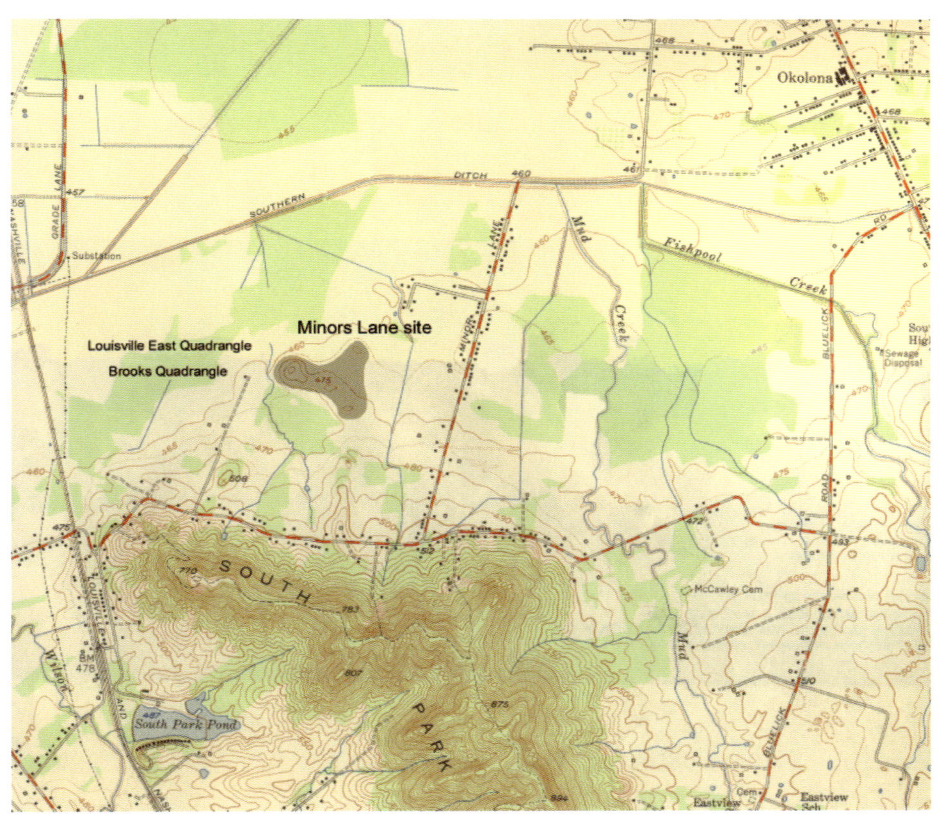

U.S.G.S. 1951 Topographic Map (Louisville East and Brooks Quadrangles)
Showing the Estimated Boundary of the Minors Lane site

The Minors Lane site was about two miles southeast of the Lone Hill site and a little further from the KYANG site. It too was located on the periphery of the Wet Woods. Like its sister sites, there was evidence of habitation from Early Archaic into Woodland times, but the period of most intense occupation was during the Late Archaic. The projectile points from the Minors Lane site are almost a carbon copy of those found at the Lone Hill and KYANG sites. What we are calling Salt River Side Nothced points were found in large numbers, as were large stemmed projectile points that could be classified as McWhinney Heavy Stemmed, or Rowlett, which are similar, if not the same.

Salt River Side Notched projectile points from the Minors Lane site

Stemmed projectile points and hafted scrapers (McWhinney Heavy Stemmed/Rowlet type) from the Minors Lane site (two artifacts to the left are hafted scrapers)

Late Archaic stemmed projectile points from the Minors Lane site

Hundreds of artifacts were found at the Minors Lane site and besides projectile points, the chipped stone inventory included drills, hafted, end and side scrapers, and preforms. From accounts of people who visited the site the author has learned that bone fragments were scattered across the site, but none were collected. If mussel shells were present they are not remembered.

The bulk of the chipped stone tools are made from cherts that naturally occur in the Knobs, and exploiting these local cherts is consistent with what was observed at the Lone Hill and KYANG sites.

Perhaps the most unusual find at the Minors Lane site was a cache of artifacts discovered by James J. Matthews. Artifact caches, although not common, have been found at the Clarksville site, and other Archaic sites in the Falls area. The cache discovered by Matthews consisted of three finely made axes and a quartz bannerstone.

Today the Minors Lane site closely resembles what it looked like fifty years ago, except for the grading that was done for construction of the Minors Lane Heights subdivision. Almost all the houses, trees and shrubs have been removed in preparation for a large commercial development.

Prehistory of the Wet Woods

From the three sites that have been discussed, parts of the prehistory of the Wet Woods are coming into focus while other aspects are still blurred. There is evidence that people have been in the Wet Woods for almost 10,000 years, but the most intense period of habitation was between 4,000 and 1,500 B.C. We are not sure what attracted people to this area, but it must have provided a resource that was either not available elsewhere, or was in a greater abundance than anywhere else. One guess is that it was a seasonal resource, like fish trapped in pools as flood waters

A cache of three axes and a bannerstone found by James J. Matthews
at the Minors Lane site

receded. Perhaps the Wet Woods was a place of refuge during those winters and early springs when there was flooding along the Ohio River and its major tributaries. During these times, game might have retreated inland and fishing and mussel collecting would have been difficult.

In Chapter 2, the botanical study of Jefferson County, Kentucky, and the adjacent counties, by Charles Gunn was cited. Gunn found that the Kentucky Scottsburg Lowland had plant communities that were not found elsewhere in the state. Perhaps plant processing tools, like pestles and nut stones, hold the answer to what attracted people to the Wet Woods. It is possible that the unique plant communities in the Wet Woods attracted deer and other game and people were drawn to the area because of the excellent hunting. The truth is that we don't know what role the Wet Woods played in the nomadic settlement pattern of Archaic people. In these situations the stock comment is that "further study is needed."

In many ways, the tool assemblages from the Clarksville site and Wet Woods sites are identical. If it were not for the large number of fishhooks and line sinkers at the Clarksville site, they could not be distinguished. The use of pebble cherts in making artifacts would be the only hint that the assemblage was from the Clarksville site. At all of these sites, Salt River Side Notched points and a variety of Late Archaic stemmed points, are the predominant spear type. The bone artifacts consist mainly of awls and needles and even the engraved motifs are similar. In terms of cultural practices, the data show a remarkable consistency in Late Archaic culture.

The site of the Minors Lane Heights subdivision after it had been cleared in preparation for commercial development. The South Park Hills are in the background.

The Miller Site

Although the Miller site was located in Harrison County, Indiana, about 30 miles southwest of Louisville, it has been considered in the general Falls area. The reason for including this site is to illustrate some of the similarities and differences among Archaic sites in the region. The Miller site was located on a terrace of the Ohio River just upstream from Mauckport, Indiana. In the late 1960s, a sand and gravel company purchased the property where the site was located and began clearing and grading the land in preparation for extensive, deep excavations. These activities exposed prehistoric cultural deposits and immediately amateur archaeologists and Indian relic collectors flocked to the site. In February, 1970, the author and two amateur archaeologists excavated a 5 by 5-foot test unit to determine the depth of cultural deposits. Test Unit A revealed a stratified site with an upper nine-inch layer of dark brown soil that contained chipped stone tools, chert waste flakes, and animal bone. Directly below this was a similar colored soil that contained a high concentration of freshwater mussel shells. This layer was also nine inches deep. It produced a smaller number of chipped stone tools and waste flakes, but there was an increase in the frequency of animal bone. The shell layer rested on a yellowish brown soil that was void of cultural material.

It was apparent that the zone of mussel shell discovered in Test Unit A was extensive because there was shell scattered over large portions of the site where grading and digging by collectors had penetrated it.

Sand and gravel operations at the Miller site in 1970

Freshwater mussel shells scattered over the surface of the Miller site

All of the artifacts from Test Unit A indicated a habitation during Late Archaic times. Small fragments of hickory nut were collected from the shell layer in Test Unit A and submitted for a radiocarbon analysis. The resulting date (recalibrated for changes in computing the date since 1970) was 4,050 B.C. Artifacts collected from the surface of the site revealed an Early and perhaps Middle Archaic occupation of the site as well, but their relatively small number probably reflects that the size of the resident population was not large, or that their stay was brief.

In May, 1970, the author returned to the site with students from Beloit College (Beloit, Wisconsin) to continue salvage operations. Destruction of the site had accelerated since Test Unit A was excavated and much of the site was now destroyed. A relatively undisturbed section was found and three more 5 by 5-foot test units (B, C and D) were excavated. These were spaced along a north-south line 110 feet long, and their purpose was to determine the extent of cultural deposits. These three units confirmed the stratigraphy found in Test Unit A - an upper dark brown soil containing cultural material (midden) over a layer of mussel shell. It also verified that this zone of buried mussel shell was extensive.

In order to get a better picture of this shell layer, one of the sand and gravel company heavy equipment operators agreed to put a bulldozer cut through the site. Although

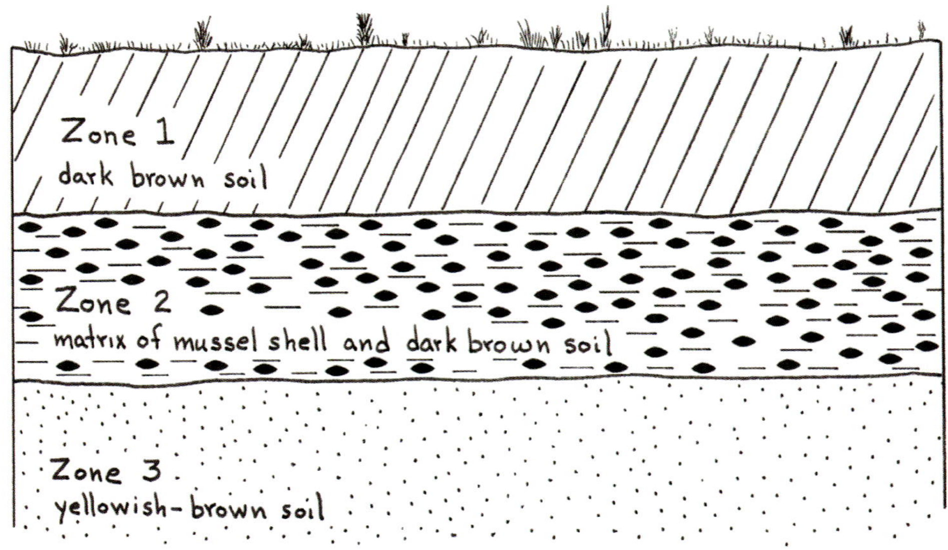

Generalized profile of the Miller site as revealed by the test units

Sidewall profile of bulldozer cut showing buried layer of freshwater mussel shells

this was destructive, the site was soon going to be destroyed anyway. A 46-foot cut through the site revealed a continuous layer of mussel shell about a foot below ground level. The thickness of the shell zone averaged around ten inches and it contained a few broken artifacts, a small number of chert waste flakes and some animal bone. Below the shell layer was a yellowish-brown soil that was void of any cultural material, animal bone, or other evidence that it was a habitation zone. In case this stratigraphy sounds familiar, it is the same as found at the KYANG site. However, at the Miller site there is no mystery as to the source of the mussel shell since the Ohio River is less than a half mile away.

We know from the stratigraphy revealed in the test units that the mussel shell layer is older than the midden deposit on top of it, but is there any difference in the artifacts associated with these two zones? The test excavations yielded a large number of midsections and tips of what were probably projectile points, but only seven whole points and one with the tip and part of the base missing. Their distribution was five from the upper midden layer and three from the mussel shell zone. Side notched points, similar to the Salt River Side Notched type, were found in both layers and probably date from the Late Archaic. It is difficult with this small sample of points to infer any significant difference in projectile point types between the upper, middle, and lower mussel shell layers. It is interesting that the long, narrow, stemmed projectile points, common at the Wet Woods sites, were missing from the test units.

Projectile points from the excavated test units at the Miller site

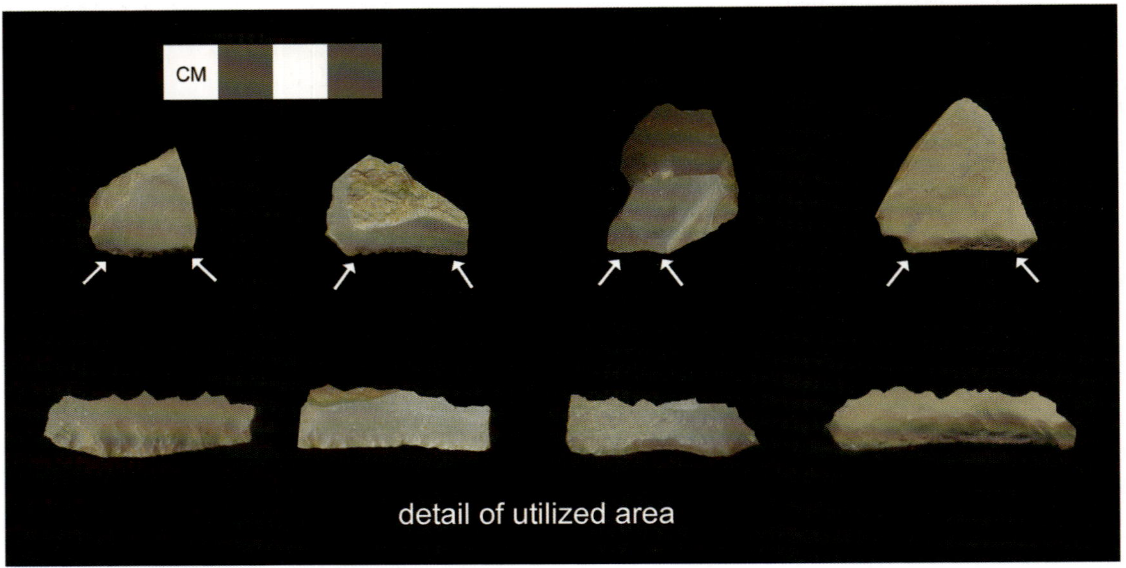

Example of utilized flakes from test units at the Miller site (utilized area is between arrows)

While the projectile points from the test units yielded limited information, another artifact that archaeologists call a "utilized flake" was more productive. A utilized flake is a waste flake that has very fine flake scars on one or more of its sides. These flake scars are so small that it seems unlikely they were intentionally chipped, and it is more probable that they resulted from using the flake to cut or scrape something. It was this cutting or scraping that produced pressure against the side of the flake and detached chips with dimensions of a millimeter of less. Utilized flakes are common at most archaeological sites, but finding them is time consuming since it requires collecting a large number of waste flakes and examining all edges on both sides of the flake.

A total of 130 utilized flakes were recovered from the Miller site test units. The vast majority of these flakes had a maximum length between one and two inches, but twelve had lengths under an inch. These "micro" tools probably had a special function that involved fine, detailed work. Two possible uses might be making mussel shell beads, or engraving designs on bone.

The stratigraphic distribution of the utilized flakes was 97 from the upper midden layer and 32 from the mussel shell zone. What makes these flakes interesting is that they were all Type III Wyandotte chert. As the reader may recall, this is a high quality gray to almost black chert that occurred in low frequencies at the Clarksville and Wet Woods sites. In contrast to these sites, the Miller site is located near some of the Wyandotte chert sources, and like the Late Archaic people at Clarksville, Lone Hill, KYANG, and Minors Lane, they were intensively utilizing the chert source that was closest to them.

The chert waste flakes from the four test units tell the same story as the utilized flakes. Before launching into this discussion the reader should be warned that quantities (one of the five things the archaeologist observes) are important, and to make sense of

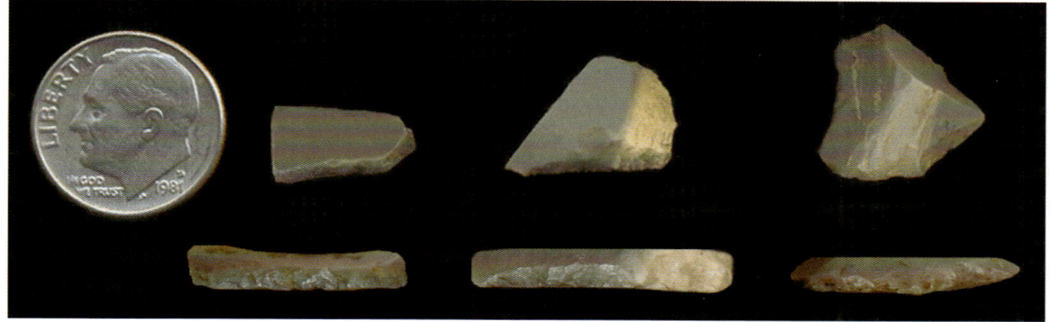

Small utilized flakes from the Miller site, with enlarged detail of flaked area

them percentages will be calculated. It is necessary to wade through the arithmetic in order to get to what archaeologists believe is the exciting part of the analysis. A total of 8,754 chert waste flakes were recovered from the test units. These were separated into groups based on chert type, and local Wyandotte chert (Type III) accounted for 97%. There were 24 pebble chert waste flakes which could have come from local sources, but obviously this chert was seldom utilized. A comparison of the number of waste flakes (by chert type) from the Miller site excavations, with those from the Clarksville site excavations, is revealing.

MILLER SITE

CHERT TYPE	NUMBER	PERCENT
Type I	201	2%
Type II	54	.6%
Type III	8,466 *	97%
Type IV	9	less than ½ %
Type V	24 *	less than ½ %

* local chert
Local cherts = 97% of the total waste flakes

CLARKSVILLE SITE

CHERT TYPE	NUMBER	PERCENT
Type I	2,244 *	10%
Type II	12,429 *	54%
Type III	933	4%
Type IV	5,308 *	23%
Type V	2,062 *	9%

* local chert
Local cherts = 96% of the total waste flakes

At both of these sites only 3% to 4% of the chert waste flakes were from non-local material, and this reinforces our hypothesis that during Late Archaic times people were primarily using locally available chert. This also suggests that the majority of flake tools of Type I and II chert found on the site were brought there as finished tools and not made on site.

Let's now consider the layer of shell as a feature and ask if we can infer any cultural differences between this zone and the upper midden layer. What we learn from the distribution of utilized flakes is that there are three times more in the midden layer than in the shell layer. All this says is that whatever the function of utilized flakes, they were being used more during the midden layer time period, which might imply that there were more people living on the site at that time. From the distribution of waste flakes we discover that in the shell layer, 99% of them were Wyandotte chert (Type III), while in the midden layer, this drops to 96%. The author considers this difference to be insignificant. The analysis of chert waste flakes found that 72% were in the midden layer and 28% in the shell zone. This could mean that with the passage of time the site population increased, or maybe the midden layer represents a longer period of time and therefore more artifacts and non-artifacts could accumulate.

The layer of freshwater mussels reflects that they were important in the diet of the early inhabitants of the site, but were not in later times. The author has no answer as to why this occurred, but suspects the answer lies more with environmental than cultural reasons. There was no evidence suggesting that a dramatic culture change occurred between the times the shell and midden layers were created. If the shells were absent it would seem as though one cultural group had been at the site all the time.

Bone preservation was excellent at the Miller site and the ground was strewn with mostly deer and small mammal bones. Some bone tools were found in the test units and these consisted mostly of the pointed ends of what were most likely awls and needles. No fishhooks, or the residuals from making fishhooks, were found.

Although the excavations did not produce any engraved bone or antler, collectors have found some excellent examples. It is interesting that the designs are

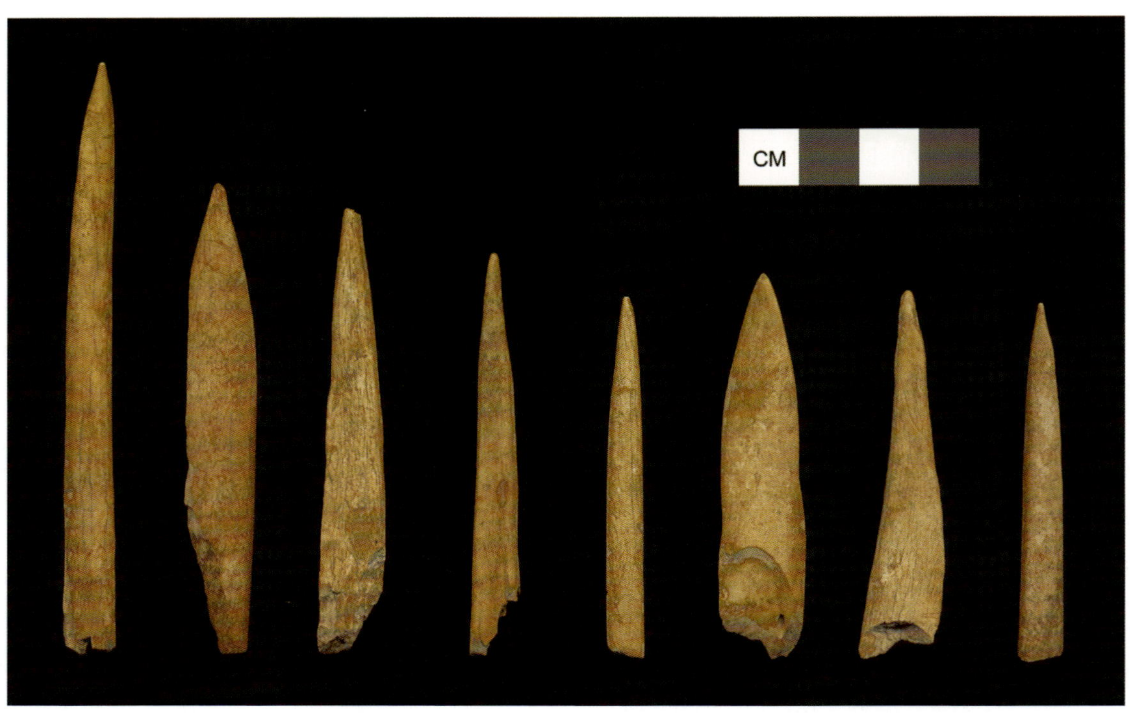

Pointed worked bone fragments from the Miller site

Rubbings taken from engraved bone artifacts found at the Miller site
(Eugene Atherton collection)

consistent with those found at the Clarksville and KYANG sites. The use of parallel lines, zig-zag and stair-stepped designs, and what the author calls the barbed-wire design, are common at both sites. It is easier to engrave designs that incorporate straight lines than curved ones, yet both the Miller and KYANG sites had examples of a continuous "S-shaped" pattern that wrapped around the bone.

In examining waste flakes from the excavations, one worked flake was found that seems like an excellent candidate for an engraving tool. The flake has been worked to a point and small flakes scars are visible with a hand-held magnifying glass. If this flake was not used as an engraver, it is what we would expect one to look like.

The Miller site produced one of the rarest artifacts from the Archaic period. It was a portion of a stone cup. This artifact is sometimes referred to as a "shotcup" since it is

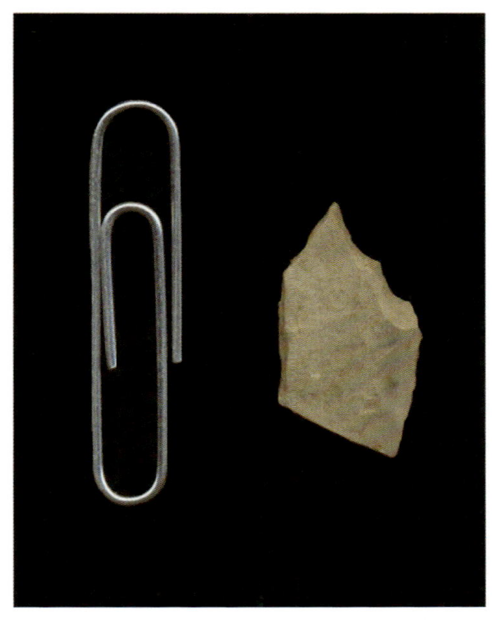

Possible bone engraving tool
from the Miller site

Three views of a stone cup fragment from the Miller site

about the size of a large whiskey shot glass. Stone cups appear to be associated with sites dating from the early part of the Late Archaic, and most of the reported finds seem to be from the Lower Ohio River and its tributaries. The Miller site specimen is made of either shale or mudstone, and even though this is not a hard substance, like quartz, it did take a craftsman to make a cup using only stone tools. The function of stone cups is not known and, to the author's knowledge, the interiors of these cups are not stained, nor is there evidence that anything has been burned in them. They may have had a ceremonial function, but this is speculation.

The reader might be disappointed that more time was not devoted to describing and picturing the artifacts from the Miller site. Archaeology is not always about finding exotic artifacts and it is certainly boring to closely examine thousands of waste flakes for signs they were utilized . . . not to mention picking them out of the screen in the field and washing them in the laboratory. However, utilized flakes and waste flakes gave us excellent information about the site and showed that there was not a dramatic change

in Late Archaic culture between the shell and midden layers.

Although Wyandotte chert was preferred for making chipped stone tools, the people at the Miller site also exploited resources in the Norman Upland (Indiana Knobs). Some chipped stone tools were made from cherts found in this region, and a hemitite pestle found on the site was from material native to the Knobs.

In this chapter all five of the things that the archaeologist observes have been used. The chert waste flakes (non-artifacts) were classified by chert type and counted. From the quantities, percentages were computed and it was found that most of the waste flakes were from local Wyandotte chert. The shell layer was considered a feature and the utilized flakes (artifacts) and waste flakes (non-artifacts) in the shell and the midden layers were separated into chert types and counted. On the basis of this empirical data it appears that other than a change in diet (eating freshwater mussels) there was no drastic change in Archaic culture. It is possible that the people who produced the midden layer had different kinds of projectile points, but we know from excavations at other Late Archaic sites in the Falls area that projectile point forms changed through time. The Miller site probably reflects the continuous development of Late Archaic culture in the Falls area.

We have examined Late Archaic sites in three of the five physiographic provinces outlined in Chapter 2. The Clarksville site at the Falls on the floodplain of the Ohio River, The Lone Hill, KYANG and Minors Lane sites in the Kentucky Scottsburg Lowland, and the Miller site on a terrace of the Ohio River in the Mitchell Plain of Indiana. If the discussion of these sites seemed to have been repetitive there is something to be learned from monotony. The Late Archaic lasts for at least 3,000 years, and while projectile point styles changed, and no doubt new groups moved in and out of the Falls area, there does not appear to have been any sudden, drastic change in culture during this time. Instead, it was perhaps a period of gradual cultural refinements and changes which led to the development of a highly efficient lifestyle based on hunting and gathering.

The Archaic period can be compared to the start of a roller coaster ride that begins with a slow, gradual, change in elevation. In archaeological terms this slow, gradual change in elevation corresponds to culture change. With the beginning of the Woodland period the roller coaster has reached the top, and what lies ahead for the next 2,500 years is an accelerated change in Native American life, and a transition that goes from small village life to living in urban centers. It is an exciting ride.

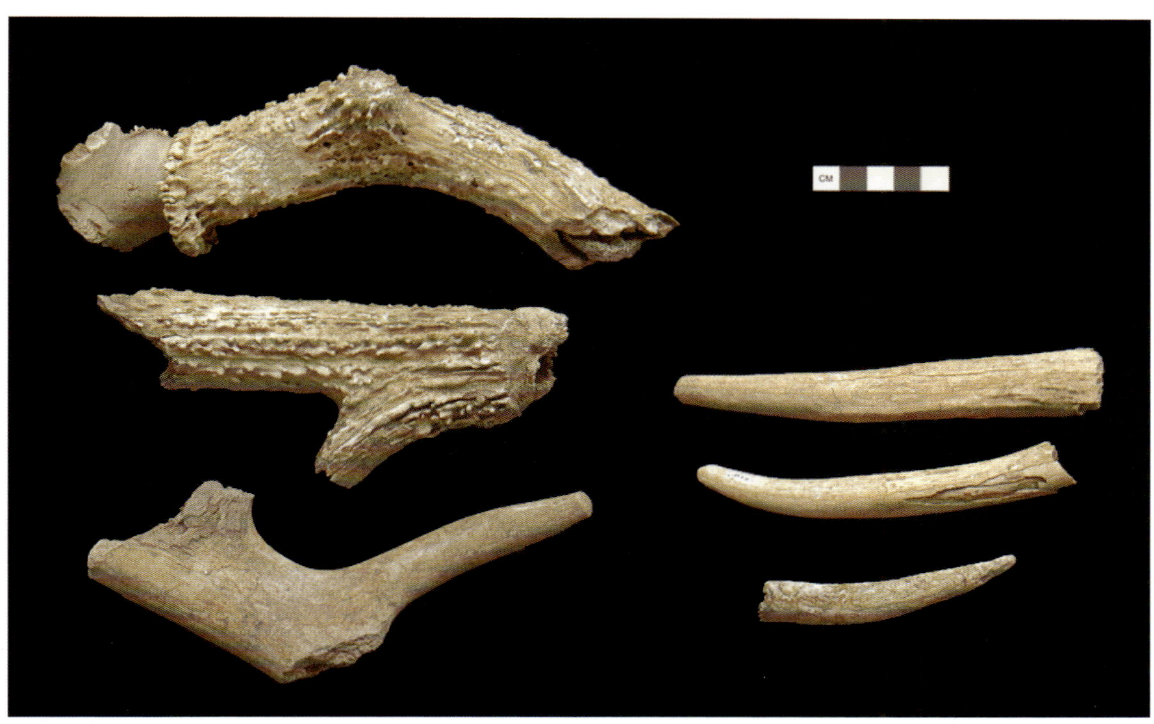

Two large deer antler fragments and four worked tines
from the surface of the Miller site

The Zorn Avenue Site

In the Falls region, the transition from the Archaic to the Woodland period occurred around 1,200 to 1,000 B.C. Compared to the Late Archaic, fewer Early and Middle Woodland period sites have been found in the Falls area and this may reflect a decline in population. The Zorn Avenue site is therefore important since it gives us a glimpse into life during that time period.

There are three things that define the Early Woodland and these involve what you eat, where you live, and containers. Put in archaeological language these are plant domestication, settled village life, and pottery. There is a saying that you are what you eat and having maize, beans and squash in your diet has a trickle-down effect through the entire culture. As anyone who has ever planted a garden knows, by August you have more tomatoes and squash than you can eat or give away. The key is that plant domestication allows for food surpluses. Hunters and gatherers must constantly exert an effort to get food, but plant domestication allows a few to produce food for many others besides themselves. This frees people from subsistence activities and in the Early Woodland we get a

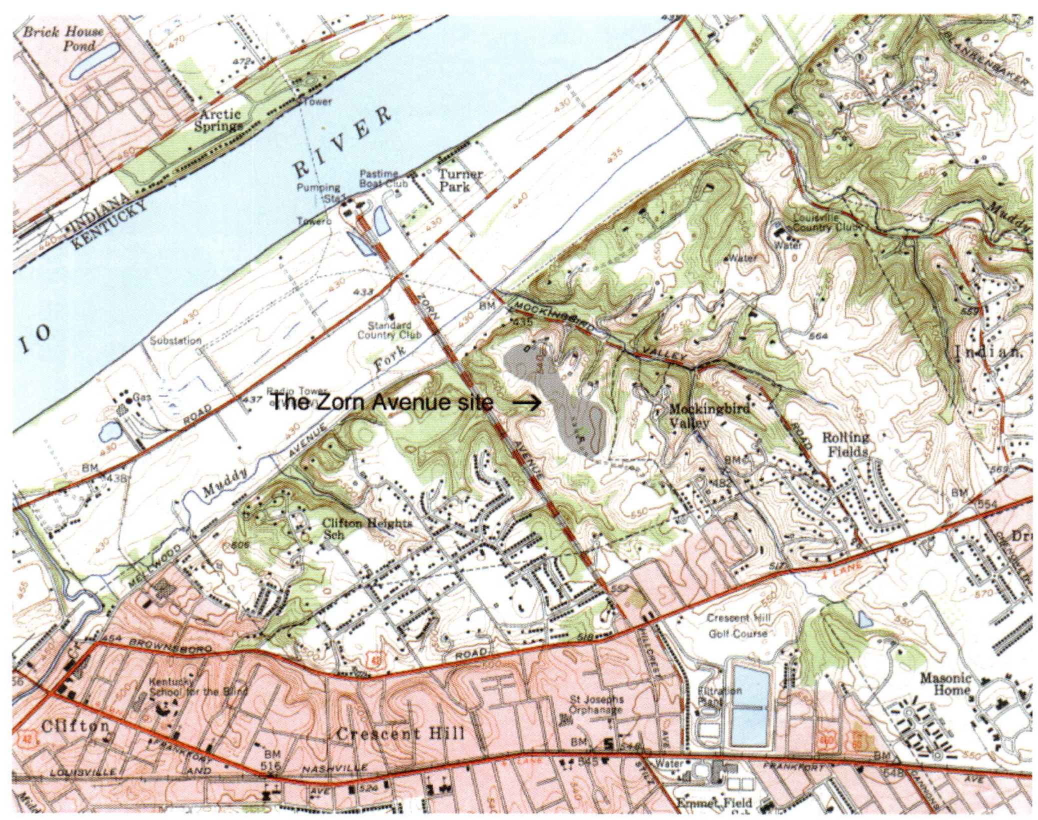

1951 U.S.G.S. topographic map showing the location of the Zorn Avenue site

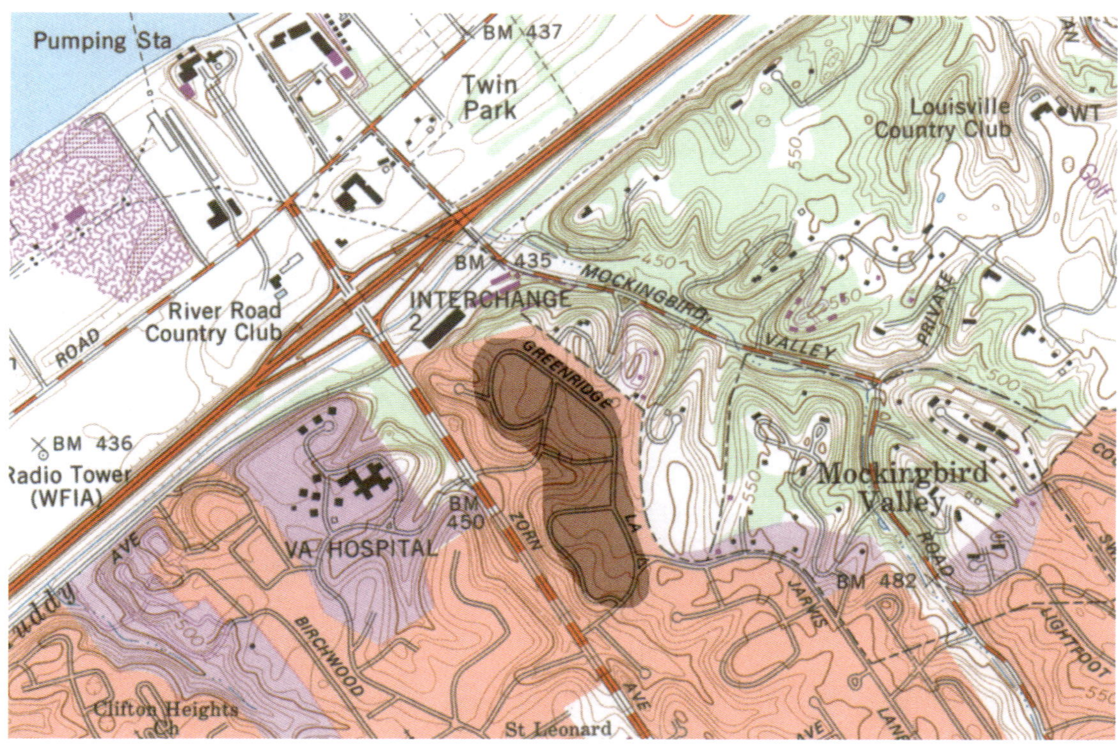

1992 U.S.G.S. map showing that portion of the Greenleaves subdivision
that impacted the Zorn Avenue site

hint of this by what appears to be craft specialization. Plant domestication also allows people to have ready access to their food, instead of having to chase after it. The result is the establishment of year-round permanent villages. We know that the first domesticated plants had their origin in Mexico, but the route they took into the southeastern United States, and when they arrived, is not exactly known. Squash appears to have been the earliest domesticated plant and initially it was merely added to the list of wild plant foods that were eaten. Pottery also takes a southern route in entering the country, and along with corn, beans, and squash, it appears suddenly in the archaeological record. In reality, the transition from Late Archaic to Early Woodland probably took several centuries, but to the archaeologist this might only be several inches of cultural deposits.

A contrast of Archaic and Woodland cultures shows some of the dramatic things that can happen when a society has a predictable food resource that can produce surpluses. From ethnographic analogy, we know that hunters and gatherers usually have egalitarian societies with decisions made by the group, or a select few. For example, the decision when to move to a new seasonal site might be made by the elders, and where to hunt by the best hunters. Status is attained by achievement or age, not acquired by birthright. With the domestication of plants, an egalitarian society gives way to one that is stratified, and we see the formation of an elite minority. This is reflected in the construction of burial mounds where a select few are laid to rest with elaborate grave goods. In this new "Mound Builder" culture, status is probably inherited and the belief system may see the beginnings of full-time specialists who conduct ceremonies, heal the sick, and are in charge of the spiritual well-being of the community.

The Zorn Avenue site was located at the top of a bluff that rose from the flood plain of the Ohio River and was east of Zorn Avenue. It is difficult to estimate the size of the site since it consisted of a northern and southern area separated by a ravine. The two areas were connected by a strip of land several hundred feet wide. It is probably safe to assume that the site covered 20 acres. It was discovered by James Matthews in the mid 1950s after heavy equipment stripped the field grasses from a large area for development of the Greenleaves subdivision. At the time, there were no professional archaeologists in the Louisville area and Matthews worked alone to salvage artifacts from the site. After several years, he had collected more than 1,000 chipped stone tools, 105 ground stone artifacts and 1725 pottery sherds. (See Bibliography for Matthews, 1958.)

A 1959 photograph looking south at the southern portion of the Zorn Avenue site after heavy equipment had removed the field grasses. On the horizon the large water tank at the Louisville Water Company plant on Frankfort Avenue can be seen.

After analyzing the artifacts he had found on the site, Matthews concluded that prehistorically the site had been occupied from Paleo-Indian to Late Woodland times, but the vast majority of the cultural material represented the Adena culture. The term "Adena" is applied to an elaborate Early Woodland culture that emerged around 1,000 B.C. and the heartland for these people was north of the Ohio River in southern Ohio and east to Charleston, West Virginia. Adena sites have been found near Lexington, Kentucky, but only a few sites west of the Kentucky River.

Some of the defining characteristics of the Adena culture are artifacts that have been found in the excavation of burial mounds. No burials were found on the Zorn Avenue site and mounds were absent. The most distinctive Adena artifact found was the rounded-base projectile points called "Adena Stemmed." These occurred with a high frequency and show that people at the Zorn Avenue site were highly influenced by groups living to the east and northeast.

In addition to Early Woodland Adena Stemmed projectile points were some typical Middle Woodland notched points. The Middle Woodland period in the central part of the eastern United States is synonymous with an elaborate culture called Hopewell, which emerged around A.D. 300. There were dual centers of this culture, one in Ohio and the other in Illinois, and from these two foci Hopewell influence spread in all directions. One interesting characteristic of Hopewell culture is artifacts made from exotic materials that are not native to the Midwest. These include copper from the Upper Peninsula of Michigan, marine shell from the Atlantic and Gulf coasts, mica from the Appalachians, and obsidian that chemical testing has identified as coming from what is today Yellowstone National Park.

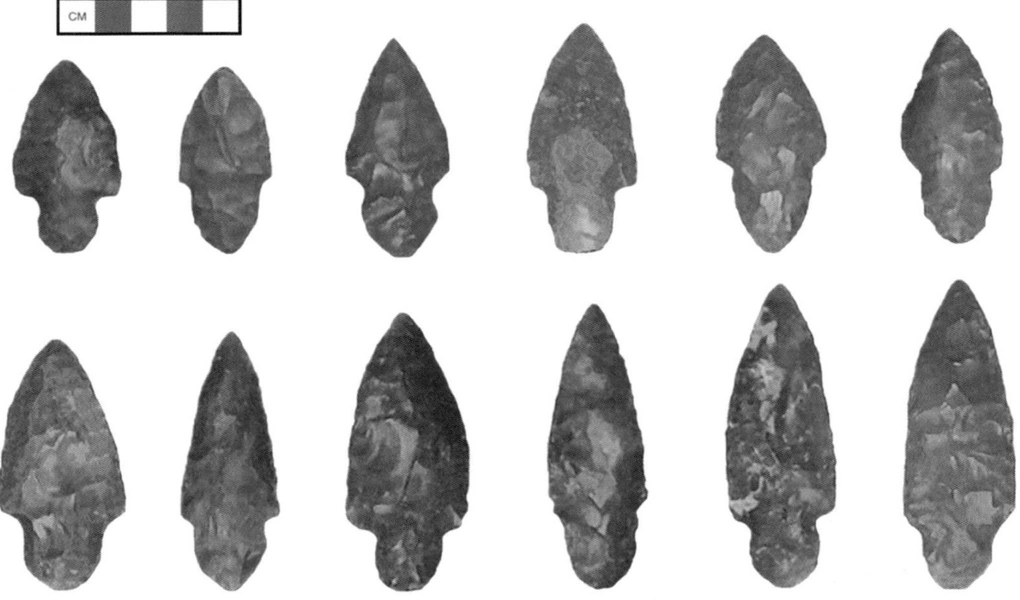

Adena Stemmed projectile points from the Zorn Avenue site
(From the James J. Matthews collection)

Hafted scrapers from the Zorn Avenue site made from Adena Stemmed projectile points
(From the James J. Matthews collection)

Middle Woodland Synders projectile points from the Zorn Avenue site
(From the James J. Matthews collection)

The use of some of these materials dates back to Archaic times and cold hammered copper awls and beads have been found at a number of sites. Copper, mica, and marine shell are associated with Adena sites, but it is during Hopewell times that the demand for these exotic materials reached a climax. Some of the items that were made include: copper beads and bracelets, marine shell cups, human and animal figures and ornamental designs carved from mica, and large obsidian blades and spears that appear to be for ceremonial purposes. Whether these goods were obtained through trade, or by expeditions to the sources, there was a sophisticated network in place that allowed them to flow into Hopewell centers. Most of these exotic materials have been found in association with burials, and both Adena and Hopewell cultures appear to have developed an elaborate mortuary complex. This points to an increasing degree of political and religious complexity where authority is in the hands of an elite few to oversee the construction of burial mounds and to supervise the system that was bringing in exotic materials that were essential to ritual and burial practices.

Adena and Hopewell cultures certainly influenced people living in the Falls area, but in a diluted way. What could be called a pure Adena or Hopewell site has not been found, but the Adena Stemmed and Snyders projectile points found at the Zorn Avenue site show this influence. In looking at the projectile points and hafted scrapers from the site, it is immediately apparent that the chert used in making chipped stone artifacts is different from that used at the Late Archaic Clarksville and Wet Woods sites. The high quality Wyandotte cherts, from deposits in Meade County, Kentucky, and Harrison County, Indiana, are preferred over cherts sources that were a short distance away. People were willing to travel thirty miles to get a high quality chert with few impurities.

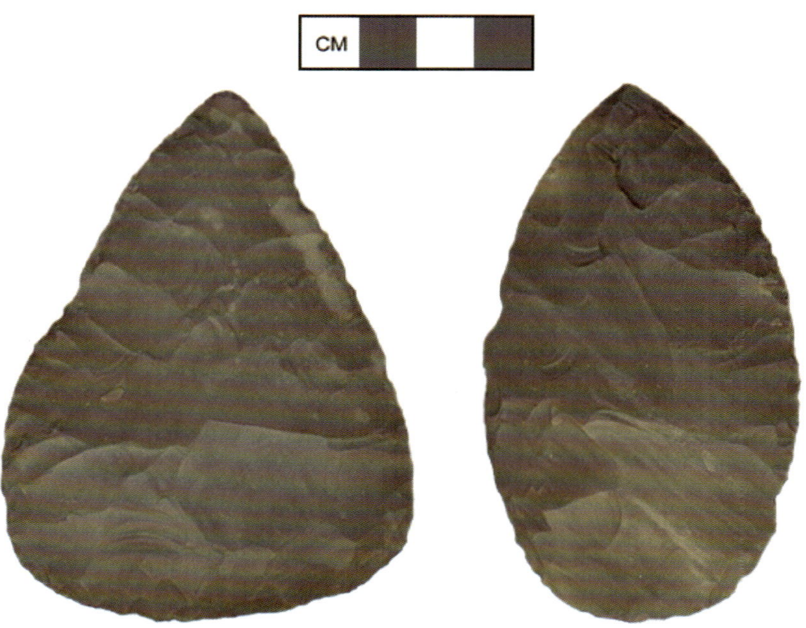

Blades made of Wyandotte chert from the Zorn Avenue site
(From the James J. Matthews collection)

A number of ground stone tools were found on the Zorn Avenue site and these included: 70 celts (whole and fragments), 8 pestles, 10 gorgets, 4 pendants, 8 hammerstones, 2 abraders, 4 nut stones, as well as fragments. A celt is a Woodland woodworking tool that in the simplest terms is an ungrooved axe. A gorget is a type of two-holed pendant. The author is not aware that any bone artifacts, or bone from food remains, were found on the site. It is assumed that bone tools were used at the Zorn Avenue site but the soil chemistry did not allow for their preservation.

Celts

Pestle

One and two hole pendants

Ground stone artifacts from the Zorn Avenue site
(From the James J. Matthews collection)

It is estimated that over 1,800 pieces of broken pottery (sherds) were recovered from the Zorn Avenue site. Like projectile points, the archaeologist loves pottery. It can be molded into a variety of shapes, various kinds of materials (temper) can be added to the clay to increase its durability, and it can painted, or have designs imprinted in the clay, before it is fired. Pottery therefore touches all three dimensions of archaeology. Some pottery has decorative motifs that are characteristic of a particular area or culture, and shapes, temper and designs change through time and allow the archaeologist to assign a relative date to a site.

Fortunately, Stephan Mocas, a professional archaeologist working in the Louisville area, became interested in the pottery from the Zorn Avenue site and devoted a considerable amount of time to analyzing it. He has classified sherds from the site into two main types, Zorn Punctate and Falls Plain. A punctate is a small depression, usually round, square, of triangular, that is put into the clay before it is fired. These can be arranged to produce a variety of patterns. By comparing Zorn Punctate with similar types from other areas, Mocas has placed it in a time period from Early Woodland into the early part of Middle Woodland. Falls Plain is a little later and dates entirely from the Middle Woodland period.

One of the unexpected things discovered at the Zorn Avenue site was features. Graders, in removing the field grasses, had exposed the tops of prehistoric fire and trash pits, which appeared as dark circular stains in the soil. At least thirteen were discovered and they averaged 31 inches in diameter and 18 inches deep. Associated with each pit were chert waste flakes, charcoal, and fragments of broken pottery. The author excavated one of these features and it contained forty Falls Plain sherds. A

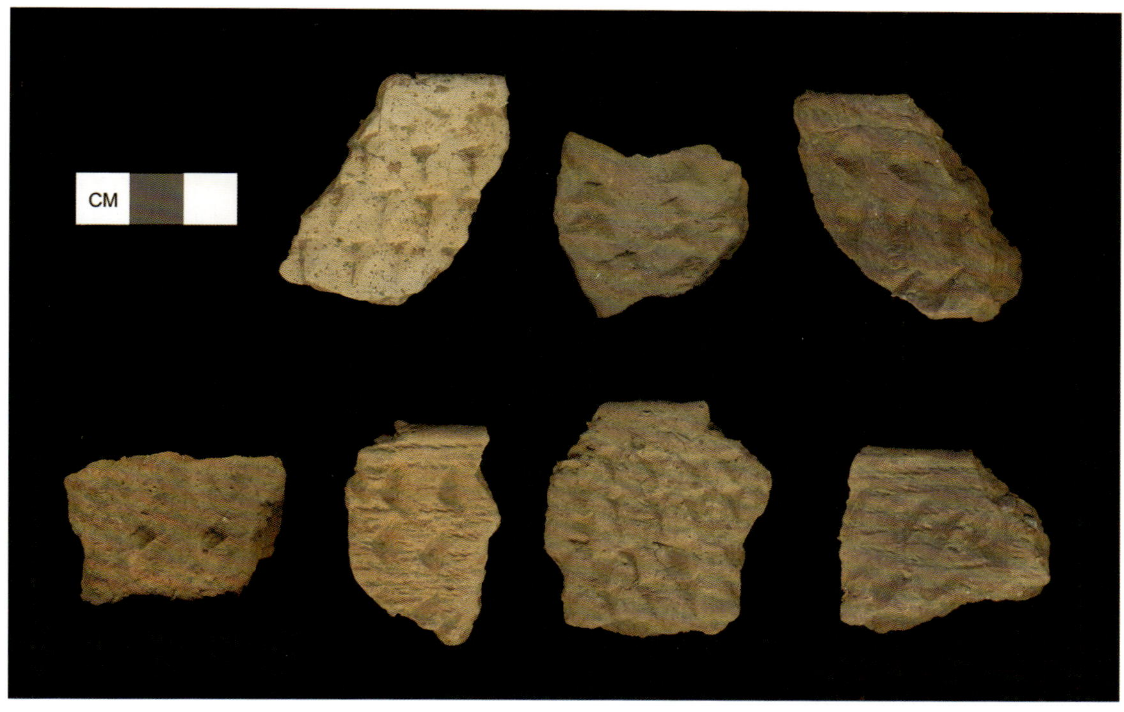

Zorn Punctate pottery from the Zorn Avenue site
(Sherds provided by Stephan Mocas)

Zorn Avenue site feature (Photo by James J. Matthews)

Falls Plain sherds excavated from a feature by the author
(Note: This pottery was tempered with crushed limestone. With time, acidity in the
groundwater leached out the temper leaving the small holes seen on the surface.)

charcoal sample from the feature was found to be contaminated, perhaps from oil that had dripped into the feature from the grader, and could not be used for radiocarbon dating.

The Zorn Avenue site represents one of those situations where we are fortunate that artifacts were collected before the site was destroyed, but frustrated that it could not have been given the attention it deserved. There is a high probability that postmold patterns from houses were present and controlled excavations could have revealed how houses were built and the layout of the settlement.

View of the Greenleaves subdivision (looking east) and a portion of the northern end of the Zorn Avenue site. A small section of Zorn Avenue can be seen in lower right and the Ohio River is visible in the upper left. (Photo by William R. Stone)

8

The Muddy Fork Site

The Muddy Fork site is of interest for two reasons, because it provides an example of a Late Woodland site, and it is a multi-component site. In discussing the Lone Hill site, for example, it was mentioned that although the main habitation was during the Late Archaic, artifacts from earlier and later periods were also found. Since the site was occupied during several time periods it is called a multi-component site. The Muddy Fork site produced cultural material that spanned 10,000 years from Early Archaic to Historic.

The Muddy Fork site was located on a hill about a third of a mile south of the intersection of Hubbards Lane with Brownsboro Road (U.S. 42). The setting is one of low, gently rolling hills, typical of the western edge of the Outer Bluegrass region.

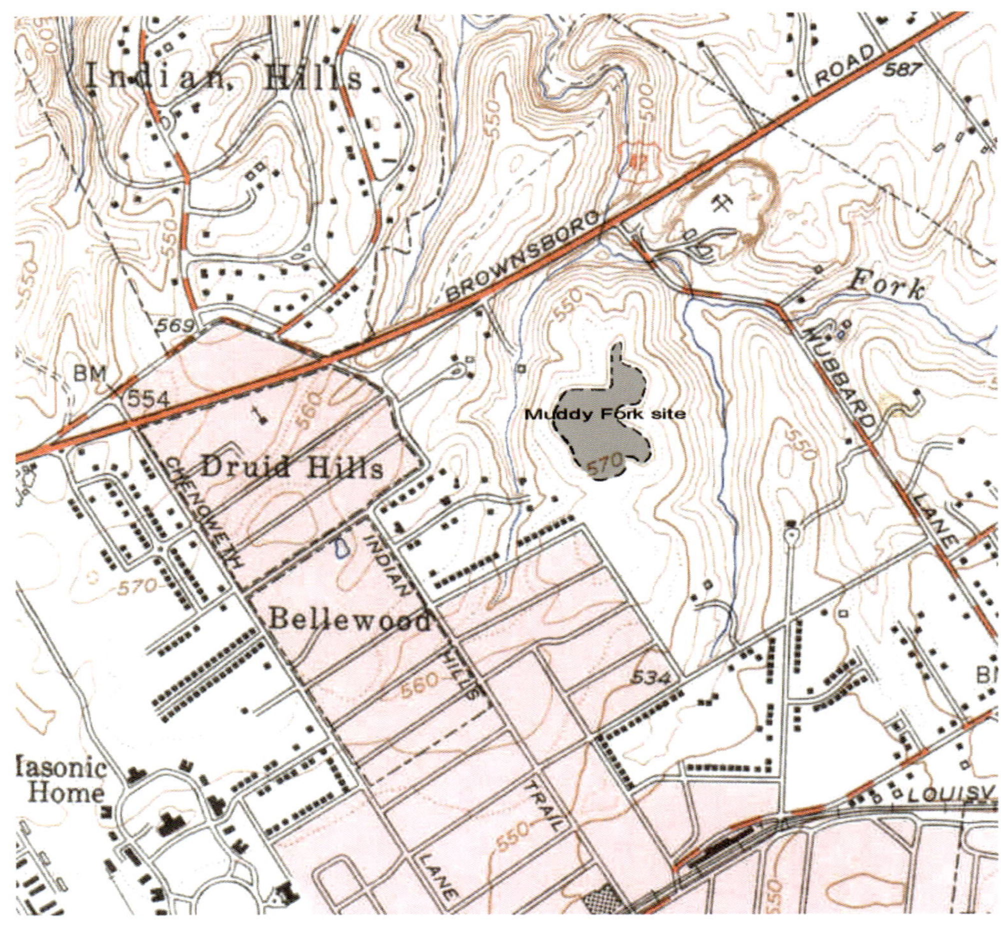

Portion of a U.S.G.S. Topographic Map (Jeffersonville, Ind.-Ky. Quadrangle 1951) showing the location of the Muddy Fork Site

The major drainage of the area is Muddy Fork, located about 1,200 feet north northeast of the site. It flows to the Ohio River which is 2.3 miles to the northwest. Two small unnamed streams enter Muddy Fork just before it goes under U.S. Highway 42.

The Muddy Fork site was discovered in 1956 when, for some unknown reason, the field grasses were stripped away. This disturbance stopped at a barbed-wire that defined a property line to the south. It is highly likely that the site was much larger and covered the entire top of the hill. The estimated dimensions of the site were approximately 500 to 600 feet north-south by 300 to 400 feet east-west.

The development of the Maryhill Estates subdivision has totally destroyed the site and grading has altered the original landscape. The best estimate for the center of the site is the intersection of Crestview Road and Yancy Lane. East of the site is a series of new office buildings and the entire area has been transformed to the degree that no one would think that it has been inhabited for 10,000 years.

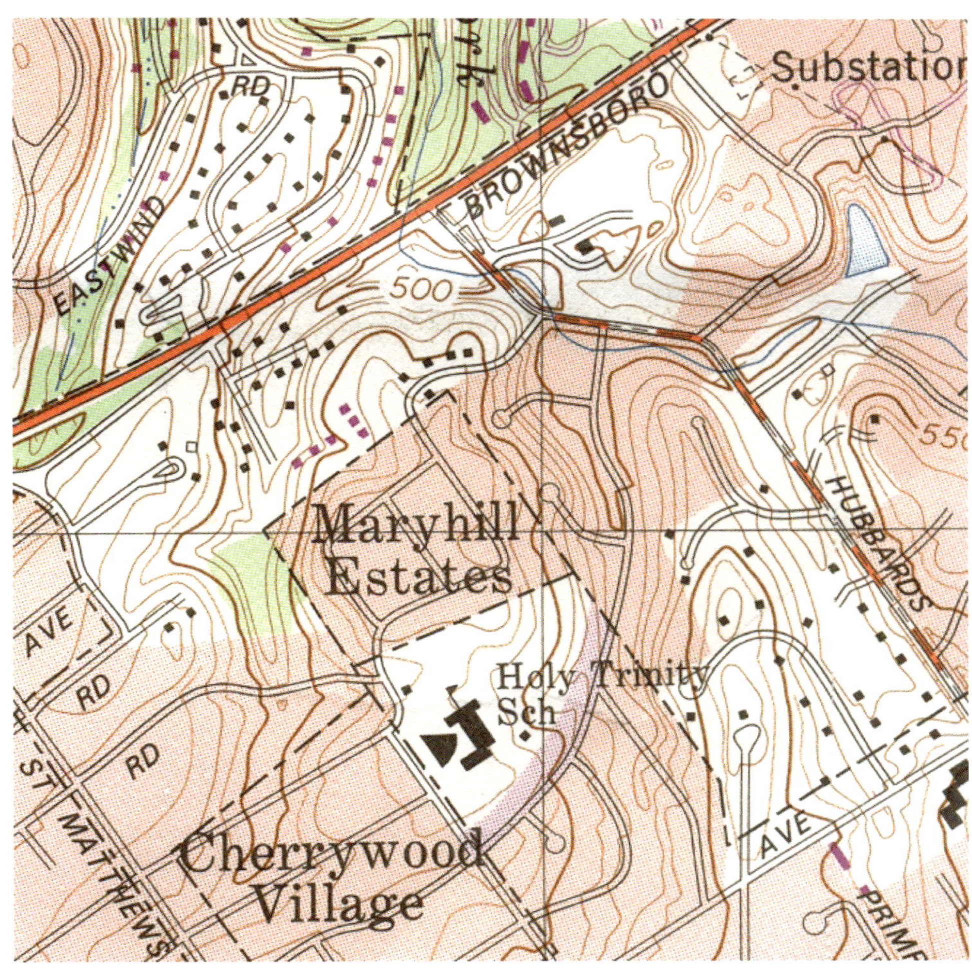

Portion of U.S.G.S. Topographic Map (Jeffersonville, Ind.-Ky. Quadrangle photorevised 1987) showing the location of the Maryhill Estates Subdivision

Muddy Fork Site Prehistoric Artifact Inventory

Chipped Stone Artifacts
Projectile and arrow points	32
Preforms	5
Drills	4
Biface fragments	35
Unifacial scrapers	4

Ground Stone Artifacts
Chert celt blade	1
Hammerstones	2
Pitted stones	1
Fragments (functions unknown)	2

Pottery sherds	696

Since grading probably exposed less than half of the top of the hill, the number of artifacts collected from the site is actually just a small sample. In addition, artifacts were collected by just one person (the author) who could only visit the site sporadically.

We will now examine each of the periods during which the Muddy Fork site was occupied. The analyses used to study the artifacts will be discussed in more detail since by this stage of the book the reader is ready for Archaeology 102. The projectile point types and dates that will be mentioned are all from the book by Noel Justice (see Bibliography).

The Archaic Period

Three projectile point types, Kirk Corner Notched, Big Sandy, and Lost Lake, tell us that the first inhabitants of the Muddy Fork site may have come as early as 8,000 B.C. These projectile point types all come from the time period of 8,000 to 6,000 B.C. A single Late Archaic stemmed point was found and this probably dates from 3,700 to 3,000 B.C. Several broken projectile points were found that appeared to be Archaic in age, but they were too fragmentary to make a positive identification. The Archaic assemblage may have included some of the scrapers and hammerstones that were found on the site. These kinds of artifacts are difficult to date since they changed little from the earliest times to European contact. What is happening at the Muddy Fork site during the Archaic period is probably the same as what we saw at the J. Graham Brown site. Hunting parties are camping along small streams during their seasonal movement to find new sources of food.

Early Woodland Period

The transition from Late Archaic to Early Woodland at the Muddy Fork site is represented by two projectile points that fall within the description of the Wade type. These points date from about 1,000 B.C. to 500 B.C., the time frame that signals the beginning of Early Woodland. One Adena Stemmed point was also found and the dates for this type are 800 to 300 B.C. All three of these projectile points were made from Wyandotte chert, which was shown at the

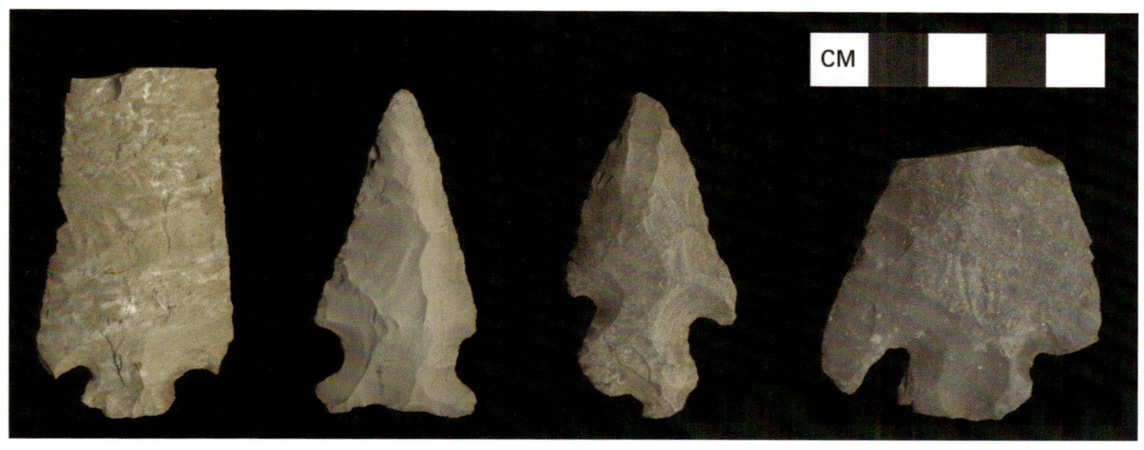

Kirk Corner Notched   Big Sandy   Late Archaic Stemmed   Lost Lake

Archaic projectile points from the Muddy Fork site

Adena Stemmed   Wade   Wade

Early Woodland projectile points from the Muddy Fork site

Zorn Avenue site to be the preferred chert type during Early and Middle Woodland times.

A large number of pottery sherds were found on the Muddy Fork site and among these were 21 plain sherds. As the description implies, there were no decorations on these sherds and they had a smooth surface. Their color ranged from reddish to brownish yellow and the average thickness was 7.6 millimeters. A distinguishing characteristic of all these sherds was one to two millimeters diameter holes on the surface. It is a standard practice in archaeology to assume that sherds pitted with holes were tempered with limestone. The reasoning is that acids in the soil have interacted with carbonates in the limestone and dissolved the temper. One of the characteristics of limestone is that it will fizz (effervesce) in the presence of an acid solution and dissolve. An examination of the holes in the plain sherds with a 20-power binocular microscope revealed that they were all rounded with sand-sized grit clinging to the sides of the clay. In several cases the cavity still had material in it that had not leached out. These holes were filled with white household vinegar to test for limestone (vinegar is a safer acid to use to test for limestone). There was no chemical reaction. Next, several small sherds were put through a washing and filtering process to extract the temper. Microscopic examination of the residue revealed a high frequency of clear, rounded crystals. A glass "scratch test" con-

firmed that these were quartz (one of the tests for quartz is that it is hard enough to scratch glass). Finally, an x-ray diffraction test of several plain sherds confirmed that the only mineral present was quartz.

From these tests it was concluded that the temper in the plain sherds was sandstone. There are some sandstones, classified as calcareous sandstone, where the glue that holds the quartz sand particles together is a carbonate. If this kind of sandstone is used as a temper in pottery, when acidic groundwater leaches out this carbonate, sand will be released, and a cavity will be left in the sherd.

The purpose of identifying the temper in these sherds is so they can be compared with similar pottery and classified. The two main types that were considered were the Early Woodland Adena plain and all its varieties, and the Middle Woodland Falls Plain

Plain pottery sherds from the Muddy Fork site

described at the Zorn Avenue site. All of the plain sherds from the Muddy Fork site were from the body of vessels so it was not possible to reconstruct the vessel size or shape. Early Woodland sandstone tempered pottery has been found at Adena sites in Eastern Kentucky, and since Falls Plain has not been reported with sandstone tempering, the author's best guess is that the Muddy Fork sherds date from the Early Woodland period.

Middle Woodland Period

Evidence of a Middle Woodland period is represented by two projectile point types, Snyders and Chesser Notched. The Snyders type, which was also found at the Zorn Avenue site, is a typical Middle Woodland projectile point and it dates during the period from 100 B.C. to around A.D. 200. By contrast, Chesser Notched points appear at the end of the Middle Woodland and continue into Late Woodland times. The dates for this type are A.D. 300-700.

During both the Early and Middle Woodland periods, evidence of habitation of the Muddy Fork site is reflected in a few projectile points and a small number of Early Woodland pottery sherds. This suggests that during this time the site was never occupied for an extended period. Although domesticated plants are now part of the diet, hunting parties still roamed the countryside and this could be one of their temporary campsites.

Late Woodland Period

The Late Woodland in the Falls area probably dates from A.D. 400 or 500 to historic times. Some archaeologists have proposed ending the Late Woodland at A.D. 1,000 and calling the next 500 years Late Prehistoric. The Muddy Fork site seems to straddle this boundary. The Late Woodland signals in the bow and arrow replacing the atlatl, and one of the defining attributes of this period is the small, triangular-shaped arrow point. Fifteen of these artifacts were found on the site and they compare favorably with Madison and Fort Ancient types. The dates for the arrow points are:

Madison   A.D.   800 - historic
Fort Ancient   A.D. 1100 - historic

Chesser Notched   Snyders

Middle Woodland projectile points from the Muddy Fork site

Arrow points from the Muddy Fork site
(Madison type, bottom and middle row, Fort Ancient type, top row)

Fort Ancient refers to a specific culture in the central Ohio Valley that came into existence around A.D. 950. The presence of Fort Ancient style arrow points at the Muddy Fork site does not mean that "Fort Ancient people" were present at the Muddy Fork site. These points imply influence from Fort Ancient in the same way Adena Stemmed points at the Zorn Avenue site implied Adena influence.

The most frequent Late Woodland artifact found at the site was pottery sherds. A total of 675 sherds dating from this period were collected, and hundreds more that had dimensions of less than a centimeter were considered too small to collect. A common characteristic of these sherds was a cord-marked exterior surface. Native American pottery was made by stacking coils of wet clay into the shape of the vessel and then pinching the coils together and smoothing the sides. In shaping the vessel and removing air bubbles from the wet clay, the sides were sometimes patted with a paddle that was wrapped with a plied fiber cord. This produced impressions of the cord in the wet clay and archaeologists refer to ceramics made this way as "cord-marked" pottery.

Cord-marked sherds from the Muddy Fork site

To examine how the cord was made, clay impressions were taken of several sherds. The first step in processing a fiber is to twist it into a strand, or "single." Next, two strands are plied together. What is called an S or Z twist will be created depending on the direction of the plying. The middle lines of these letters describe the direction of the twist. Most of the cord markings on the Muddy Fork sherds were weathered, but several good positive impressions were obtained and they showed an S twist.

No sizable sherds were found at the Muddy Fork site so it was not possible to determine vessel shape or size. The average thickness of the sherds was about a quarter of an inch. Only eight sherds displayed a form of decoration and these consisted of incised lines and punctates (intentionally impressed holes). On one sherd two incised lines formed a "V" and on another they made an "X". It is speculated that a diamond pattern might have existed. Three sherds had small punctates that were only a millimeter or two in diameter. On first inspection it was thought that these were caused by erosion of the surface, but on closer examination, on one sherd there were bulges on the inside the sherd opposite the holes. This means that the holes were made before the pot was fired and were therefore intentional.

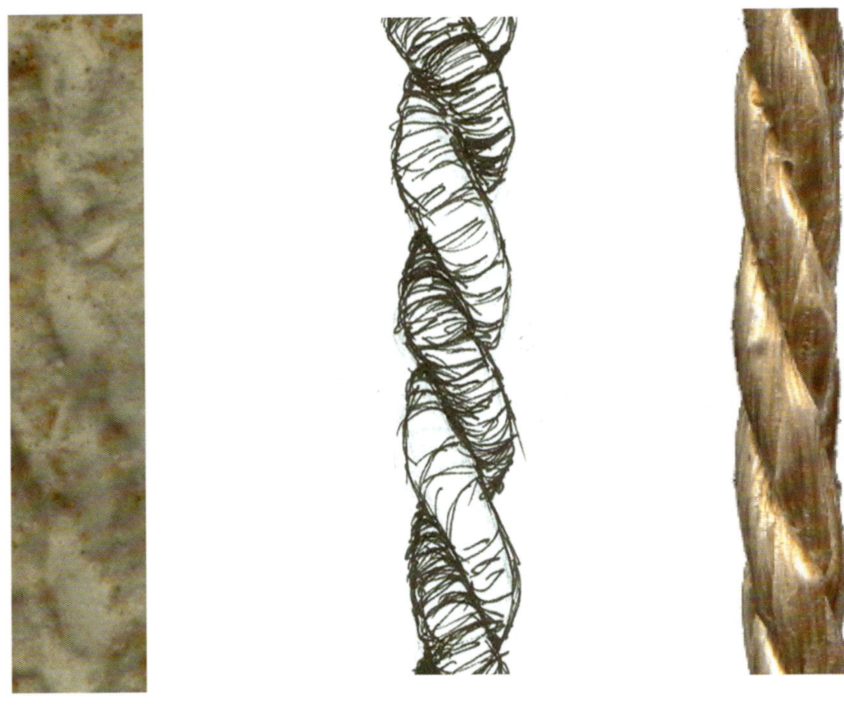

Clay impression from sherd   Sketch of S-Twist   S-Twist cord

Clay impression of Muddy Fork sherd with drawing and example of S-Twist cord
(Drawing by Leigh Bader)

Decorated sherds from the Muddy Fork site
(Incised sherds - bottom row,   Punctated sherds - top row)

In making pottery, Native Americans added a temper to the clay to serve as a bonding agent. A variety of materials were used as temper and some of the common kinds were crushed stones (grit temper) and pulverized mollusk shells. Archaeologists are interested in temper because it can be an indicator of when and where the pottery was made. It was decided to dissolve several of the Muddy Fork cord-marked sherds and examine its temper to see exactly what kind of rock was being used. At the time it was not known that this would produce surprising results.

The process of extracting the temper involved repeatedly soaking and breaking a sherd and then filtering the solution. Eventually this resulted in a residue of fine stone particles and these were placed on a white surface and examined with a 20-power binocular microscope. The temper was collected with tweezers and placed in a small plastic container. As this was being done it was noticed that the temper adhered to the tweezers. It was magnetic! A magnet was placed in the vicinity of the temper that had been collected and it all clung to the magnet. This was not expected since no other case could be found in the archaeological literature where a sherd had ever displayed magnetic properties.

The entire assemblage of cord-marked sherds from the Muddy Fork site was tested for magnetism and it was possible to separate them into three classes; (1) those that adhered to a magnet, or could be moved with a magnet, (2) those that could not be moved by a magnet but caused the needle of a compass to move, and (3) those that showed no apparent magnetic properties. Two-thirds of the sherds either adhered to a magnet or could be moved by a magnet, about a third moved the needle of a compass, and only two sherds displayed no apparent magnetic properties.

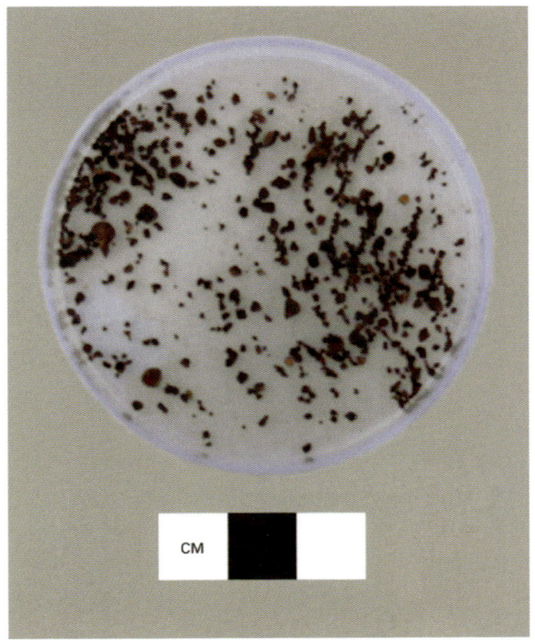

Magnetic temper from cord-marked sherd

Cord-marked sherd adhering to magnet

As usually happens when research answers one question, several more appear. The temper used in the Muddy Fork cord-marked pottery is magnetic. What is this material? Magnetite is the most naturally occurring magnetic mineral, but an x-ray diffraction analysis of the temper could only identify it as a weathered rock that had undergone chemical changes.

Where Native Americans were getting this magnetic material was an easier question to answer. Stream beds are a ready source of sand and gravel so Muddy Fork, in the vicinity of the site, was inspected. A hand-held magnet was passed over some exposed gravels and immediately it was covered with small pieces of angular gravel. These were observed with a 20-power binocular microscope and appeared identical to the temper extracted from the cord-marked sherds. An x-ray diffraction analysis produced identical results, as found in the analysis of the temper. There is the possibility that the magnetic material was in the clay deposits that were used to make the pottery, but if this were the case it would seem logical that other kinds of rock would also be present. Until clay deposits with a high content of magnetic material, and no other rocks, are found, it is logical to conclude that this material was derived from Muddy Fork, or other streams in the area.

Muddy Fork in the vicinity of the Muddy Fork site

At the end of Chapter 3 on the J.Graham Brown site is a photograph of a Late Woodland cord-marked sherd. When this sherd was tested for magnetic properties it clung to the magnet. Gravels in the Middle Fork of Beargrass Creek, which borders the J. Graham Brown site to the south, were tested with a magnet and, like Muddy Fork, contained magnetic gravels. Because of the discovery of magnetic pottery at the Muddy Fork site, some archaeologists are now taking magnets with them in the field and testing pottery. Two other sites, one in southern Jefferson County, Kentucky, and another on a terrace of the Ohio River in Floyd County, Indiana, have produced magnetic pottery.

The Historic Period

In addition to the prehistoric components at the Muddy Fork site, there was also an historic one. A total of eleven Civil War period bullets were found on the site and four different calibers were represented. The caliber and number of bullets are:

.58 caliber minie ball	4
.58 caliber Williams Type III	4
.52 caliber Spencer	2
.36 caliber pistol ball	1

None of the bullets are severely dented or flattened, which suggests they had not been fired. If the pistol ball was fired, it does not appear to have hit anything.

Two other historic artifacts found on the site were a small cast iron object and a fragment of a glazed clay pipe. The cast iron artifact has a scroll decoration and appears to be a handle that was attached to something. Since the object is decorated it was probably used with some personal item, such as a riding crop or baton. It is logical to infer that since both of these items are associated with Civil War period bullets, they probably date from the same period.

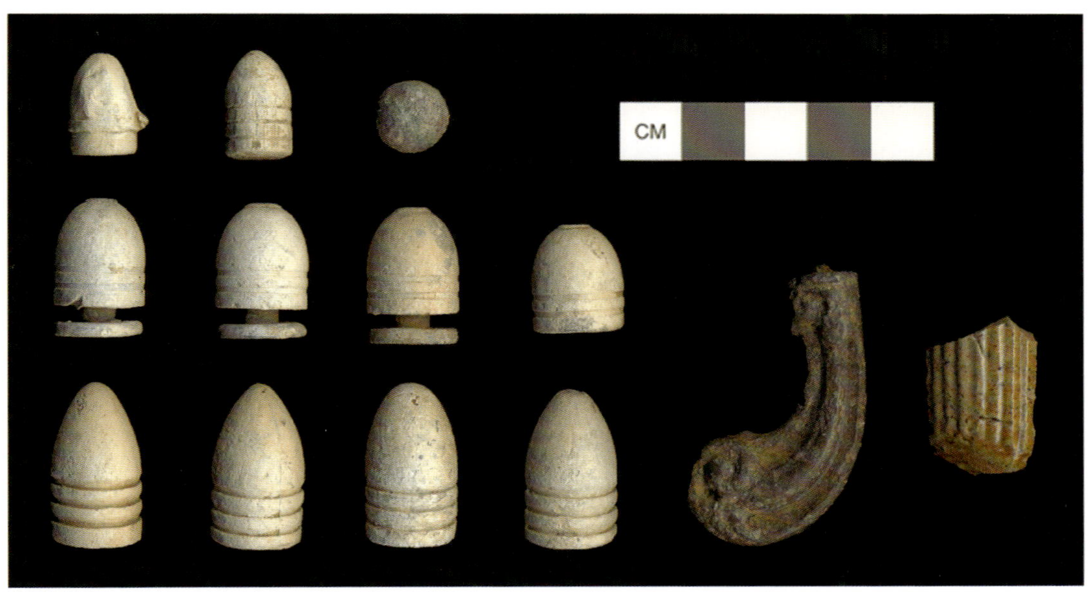

Civil War era artifacts from the Muddy Fork site
(Bottom row of bullets, 58 caliber minie ball, middle row, .58 caliber Williams Type III, top row, two 52 caliber Spencer bullets and .36 caliber pistol ball, cast iron object and clay pipe fragment lower right)

CIVIL WAR ERA BULLETS AND BALLS

A .58 caliber minie ball was not really a "ball" but a kind of shell invented by Claude E. Minie. They were usually fired with a Springfield rifle.

A .58 caliber Williams Type III shell was a type of "self-cleaning" bullet.

A .52 caliber Spencer bullet was fired with a 7-shot carbine and these were used primarily by cavalrymen.

A .36 caliber ball was used in a handgun, not a rifle.

From the type of bullets that were found, it appears that this was a Union camp. No historic records were found that would date when troops were on the Muddy Fork site, but the small number of artifacts that were recovered implies that it was a temporary encampment and may have been used for reconnaissance purposes.

Today the Muddy Fork site is covered with suburban homes and nearby is a major four-lane highway. It is difficult to imagine that at one time it was a camping site for hunters who used an atlatl, people who made simple clay pottery and hunted with a bow and arrow, and Civil War soldiers. In prehistoric times the tributaries of the Ohio River served as early highways for prehistoric people and hunters followed these to the interior to hunt for game. One route was

Looking southwest across Brownsboro Road (U.S. 42) at the Maryhill Estates and the location of the Muddy Fork site

Beargrass Creek and its tributary, Muddy Fork. The Muddy Fork site was an ideal place to establish a temporary camp and there were probably hundreds of similar camps along Beargrass Creek and its tributaries. Sites that were inhabited for a long period of time produce thousands of artifacts. Since relatively few artifacts were found at the Muddy Fork site, it is inferred that it was usually a temporary camp site. Only during Late Woodland times did this probably change and the presence of hundreds of pottery sherds implies that there was some permanence to the habitation at this time. If excavations had been conducted, the remains of small houses would probably have been found.

When the Muddy Fork site was walked in the 1950s it was not known that it could possibly be significant. Its significance lies in having introduced the archaeologist to pottery with magnetic properties that has now been found on four different prehistoric sites in the Falls area.

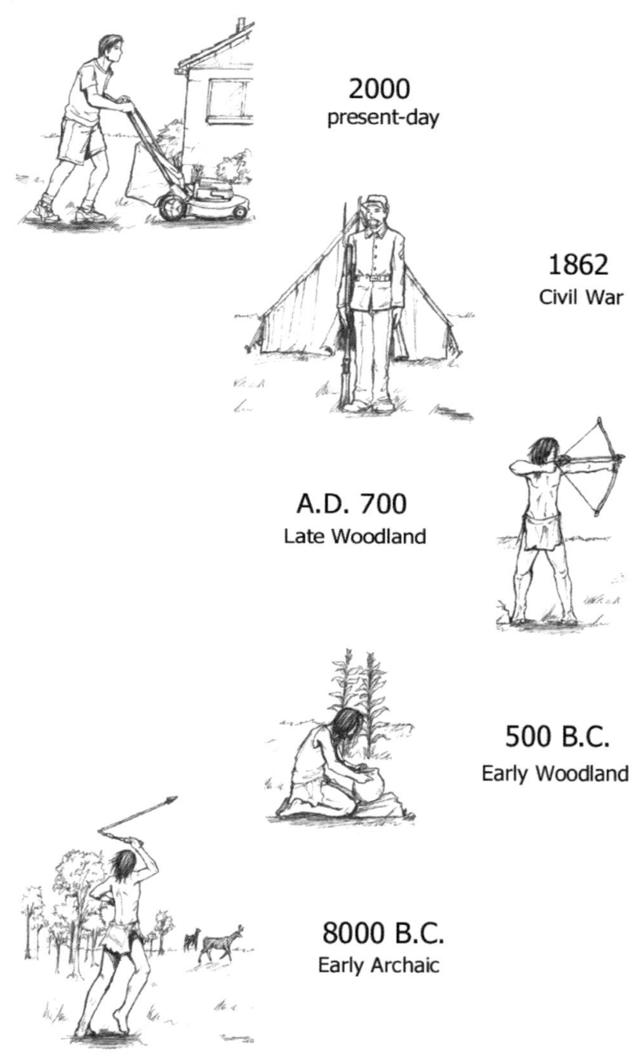

10,000 years of living on the Muddy Fork site.
(Drawings by Leigh Bader)

Closing Remarks

The author hopes the reader has enjoyed this 10,000-year trek from the Early Archaic period at the J Graham Brown site to a Civil War encampment on the Muddy Fork site. No doubt you thought that the Archaic would never end as site after site dated from this period. Yes, the Archaic lasted a long time and no doubt there were children getting up in the morning at the Clarksville and Lone Hill sites and asking their parents, "Is it Early Woodland yet?" Most likely by this stage of the book your vocabulary has been expanded to include the word "chert", and some of you may now be comfortable saying "riverine environment" and "molluscan fauna." What has been presented in this book is merely the tip of the prehistoric iceberg in the Falls of the Ohio River region. The records of the Kentucky Heritage Council list more than 600 prehistoric archaeological sites in just Jefferson County, Kentucky, and it is tempting to speculate that at least this many have unknowingly been destroyed by residential and commercial development.

Perhaps a warning should be issued to the reader not to take the interpretations that have been made as fact. There will always be disagreements among archaeologists on how the data should be interpreted, and they will certainly exist here. As an example, some archaeologists consider chert waste flakes to be artifacts. In this book they have been classified as non-artifacts, like sawdust from cutting a board. Whether they are artifacts or non-artifacts hardly seems worth debating. The important thing is that they are data. The classification of prehistoric periods that has been used starts with Paleo-Indian and ends with Late Woodland and Mississippian. A number of archaeologists are now adding Late

Prehistoric as the final phase that comes between Late Woodland and European contact. There are advantages to adding this phase, although a search of the literature indicates that it is not universally accepted. Since none of the sites discussed in this book date from that period, it could be confidently avoided.

The author has intentionally painted the picture of the sites discussed in this book with a broad brush. At all five of the Archaic sites that were described, some Early Archaic projectile points, like those at the J. Graham Brown site, were found. In addition, there were also representative points from the Woodland period. Prehistoric people have been wandering over this region for 10,000 years and "Do Not Trespass" signs were not posted when a group left a site. The artifacts that have been pictured were selected as representative examples of the time period when the major occupation of the site occurred.

An attempt has been made to weave the first chapter, Archaeology 101 for the Public, into the discussions and interpretations that have been proposed. It is important to remember the three kinds of evidence that were outlined; (1) empirical or observable, (2) logical, and (3) speculative or intuitive. These terms have been used frequently so the reader will know which interpretations are highly probable and which ones are guesses. This should be remembered because what follows in this chapter is the author's attempt to move from being an archaeologist to an anthropologist and talk about prehistoric culture. It is important to move beyond descriptions and comparisons, and to put meat on the skeleton that has been created by looking at artifacts, non-artifacts, features, associations, and quantities.

The sites whose main period of habitation was during the Late Archaic period were in three different geographical areas. The Clarksville site was on the flood plain of the Ohio River, the Miller site in the Mitchell Plain, on a terrace overlooking the Ohio River, and the Lone Hill, KYANG, and Minors Lane sites were inland and adjacent to the Wet Woods area in the Kentucky Scottsburg Lowland. Although these sites were in different areas, they all had a common cultural signature. There were tools for killing, cutting, processing, scraping, drilling, hammering, puncturing and sewing. They had similar items of personal adornment, and the designs engraved on bone tools were the same. It made no difference if the site was at the Falls, adjacent to the Wet Woods, or on a terrace overlooking the Ohio River, people took time to make that special item, the bannerstone. This constellation of artifacts reflects that similar kinds of activities were taking place at each site.

Archaic people relied on hunting and gathering for their food and this meant they were nomadic. They knew about the Wet Woods, the Falls and its food resources, and were aware of natural resources that could be found in the Knobs and Norman Upland. In the first chapter there was a short section on Culture and the Environment, and the Archaic period serves as a good example of the interplay of these two systems. While the environmental setting of the Falls area provided abundant food resources, their availability fluctuated during the year. As a way of maximizing these resources, groups culturally adapted and would move their settlement inland, or to the Ohio River, to exploit seasonal opportunities to hunt, fish, and gather plant foods. Archaeologists refer to this as a shifting settlement pattern.

Another kind of cultural adjustment might have been to locate a settlement near the juncture of several geographical areas. This could have reduced the amount of seasonal movement and, with the abundant food resources in the Falls region, maybe a residual population could remain at a site for the entire year. Usually hunters and gatherers do not have year-round settlements, but there are exceptions. The Tareumiut, coastal Alaskan Native Americans, provide a good example. This group moves seasonally with the availability of whales, sea mammals, and aquatic birds. Once the whaling season is over in late spring, groups will leave the home village for the summer to go inland to hunt, or to fish and hunt water foul along the coast. Although most of the population leaves at this time, the village is not abandoned and the elderly, children and some young adults will remain. If there are sufficient resources to support year-round villages among the Tareumiut, it should have been possible in Late Archaic times in the Falls of the Ohio River region where there were abundant natural resources.

It is tempting to speculate on the size of the Late Archaic groups in the Falls area. People studying modern-day hunters and gathers (ethnographers), have found that estimating population size is difficult since these groups are constantly moving, and either breaking apart, or coalescing into larger units. One study of the inland Nuunamiut hunters of Alaska actually counted the number of people in seasonal camps and found it varied from 10 to 20 persons. The number increased dramatically when groups came together and in 1885, a base camp was estimated at 225 people.

The Siriono of Eastern Bolivia are hunters and gatherers that are organized into bands and the size of a band ranges from 30 or 40 to as many as 120 persons. The excavations at the Clarksville site showed that there were a variety of reliable food resources available at the Falls of the Ohio River and these included deer, fish and freshwater mussels. Based on the size of Nuunamiut and Siriono groups, it seems logical to estimate that at certain times of the year the Clarksville site could have easily supported 100 or more persons.

There are some interesting problems that still puzzle archaeologists and one of these is the sudden disappearance of mussel shells in Late Archaic cultural deposits. Examples of this were seen at the KYANG and Miller sites, and it exists at other Late Archaic sites as well. It is as if freshwater mussels were suddenly no longer part of the diet. This is, of course, reading the archaeological record too literally, but it does appear to have happened quickly. From the perspective of the culture, it could have happened over two or three generations. It is probably safe to assume that Late Archaic people did not consciously decide to stop eating mussels. Food taboos do occur in societies, but for hunters and gatherers to stop a practice that had lasted for generations does not seem logical. Another possibility is that a new group of people moved into the Falls area and they did not eat mussels. To the author this is also not logical.

There are a number of factors that can lead to the reduction of freshwater mussel populations. Besides over-collecting by humans, mussels are part of the diet of animals such as muskrat, racoon and mink, and the freshwater drumfish. Mussel beds can also be harmed by harsh winters and sediments building up after a flood. Speculating on the human factor in this equation is tempting. If there are 50 persons at a site, and each person eats ten mussels a day for 200 days, this is 100,000 mussels. Add to this the mussels eaten by small animals and fish, and throw in a harsh winter or bad flood every decade, and it seems possible that a

mussel bed could be depleted to the point where it was not worth exploiting. It was probably a combination of factors, but over-exploitation by people may be at the head of the list. Remember, this is speculation.

Since Archaic times, artifacts were made from material such as copper, the source of which was some distance away. In the Falls area, there are beads and awls made from copper, and the closest source is Michigan's Upper Peninsula. The presence of fired clay objects at the Clarksville site, identical in appearance to those found at a site in Louisiana, hint at some kind of interaction between these two areas.

In the Middle Woodland, the flow of exotic items into Hopewell centers is impressive. How did marine shell from the Atlantic and Gulf coasts, mica from the Appalachians, and copper from Michigan's Upper Peninsula find its way to Ohio and Illinois? An even bigger mystery is how obsidian, in large quantities, got to these areas from what is today Yellowstone Park. Archaeologists do not have answers to all of these questions, so again we turn to speculation. Were there Hopewell equivalents of the Lewis and Clark expedition sent to get these exotic materials? Were there extensive trading networks between adjacent groups? There are various possibilities to explain how items from far away were obtained. Regardless, if it were by directly going to the source or through trade, there are data to suggest that there were obstacles to overcome. These data are languages. Linguists have been studying Native American languages for over a hundred years and during that time they have been lumped and split into various classifications. It is probably safe to estimate that at the time of European contact there were over forty distinct languages east of the Mississippi River, and counting known languages that are not sufficiently documented to classify, the number could be closer to seventy. Long-distance travel and trade in prehistoric times meant crossing many different language areas. The fact that obstacles like these could be overcome is a testimony to the effectiveness of the Hopewell political and economic systems.

Around A.D. 400 to 500 the elaborate cultural trappings of Middle Woodland Hopewell culture start to diminish and in the midwestern states there is a transition to the Late Woodland period. Burial mounds start to disappear and the network that was responsible for bringing copper, mica, marine shell and obsidian into the region fades away. Late Woodland sites seem to be small horticultural settlements and there is a tendency to think that this represents a cultural decline. Just because exotic artifacts are no longer buried with the dead and the belief system seems to have changed does not equal a decline. We do not say that a small rural town with a frame church has less of a belief system than a city with a great cathedral.

Hopewell culture seems to culminate in an elaborate mortuary practice that began in Early Woodland times. If we think of culture as an integrated system composed of social, economic, political, and religious parts, a change in one of these can have a ripple effect through the whole culture. Perhaps the decline of Hopewell culture was a breakdown in the belief system, and once this was peeled away and the social, economic and political parts readjusted, what was left over were Late Woodland horticultural villages. There was still a strong culture, but it had changed.

In the Falls region it appears that there was a gradual evolution from the Early to Late Woodland. This area only tangentially participated in the Adena and Hopewell cultures and during this time there was probably an increasing dependency on domesticated plants and the development of efficient ways to grow and manage crops. We should not think of this occurring in isolation from other groups. An exchange of ideas probably flowed throughout the Ohio River valley and it is certainly possible that groups moved in and out of the area.

The Muddy Fork site is probably a good example of a Late Woodland site in the Falls area. The site did produce one surprise, pottery with a temper that was magnetic. To the author's knowledge, the use of magnetic temper in Late Woodland pottery has never been reported. It appears this material came from creek gravels. We move into the realm of speculation when considering how this magnetic material was obtained. If a handful of gravel is randomly collected from Muddy Fork or Beargrass Creek it will most likely contain some of this magnetic material, but if it is used as temper it will not be in a concentration that is high enough to magnetize pottery. Since this magnetic material is denser than other creek sands and gravels it can be sorted by stream action and occur in concentrations. One possibility is that such concentrations were accidently selected as the source of temper. The problem with this assumption is that since this study was done pottery with magnetic temper has now been found at four sites. It seems unlikely that it accidently occurred four times. This suggests that it was intentional, not a random, selection of temper.

There is a behavioral difference between randomly scooping up creek gravels for temper and intentionally selecting specific gravels that cannot be identified with the naked eye. How were Native Americans able to do this? Is it possible that they knew about lodestones? This is the common name given to magnetite, which is a naturally occurring magnetic mineral. Was this natural magnet used to collect the temper from stream beds? If so, why was it important to use this material as a temper? Did its iron content allow the pottery vessel to retain heat longer? We are deep into speculation at this point. The archaeological literature that the author has searched does not mention a lodestone having ever been discovered at an archaeological site. Since a lodestone would look like a common rock, and archaeologists do not carry magnets to test the magnetism of rocks, this may be the reason one has never been found. It seems logical to assume that more sites with magnetic pottery will be discovered in the future. So again we use that catch-all phrase, "More research is needed."

The prehistoric developmental sequence for the Eastern United States has traditionally started with Paleo-Indian and ended with Late Woodland and Mississippian. Mississippian refers to a cultural manifestation, contemporary with Late Woodland/Late Prehistoric, that originated in the Southeastern states and spread northward up the Mississippi River and its major tributaries. Some archaeologists are now ending the Late Woodland at A.D. 1,000 and adding Late Prehistoric as the last period before European contact. This is a difficult period to define objectively and it seems to be based on degrees of change that took place in the evolution from small Late Woodland horticultural settlements to large agricultural villages.

Based on our current level of understanding from Late Woodland times, maybe until European contact, the Falls of the Ohio River served as a point of intersection between upstream and downstream groups. Several large Mississippian sites are documented in the Falls area and archaeologists are trying to understand the dynamics that occurred when they encountered the late period agriculturalists living in the area. It appears to the author that the nature of this interaction is being studied primarily through detailed comparisons of each group's pottery. In the books and articles that the author has read on this subject, seldom, if ever, are there references to studies in cultural anthropology. Cultural anthropologists have looked at how different groups interact and this should be of interest to archaeologists working with late period sites. For example, from his study of small Mexican communities, cultural anthropologist Robert Redfield realized that these communities were really not isolated but had to be viewed in a larger context. Redfield coined the terms "Great" and "Little" tradition to study the interaction between urban ("Great") and rural ("Little") communities. He noted that although rural communities maintain their folk traditions, they still interact with urban centers and absorb some of their culture. It seems to the author that Redfield has suggested a model that could be used in the Falls area for looking at the interaction between the urban-like Mississippian culture and the rural Late Woodland/Late Prehistoric cultures.

When there is an interaction between different cultures, looking at the material culture can send confusing signals. An anthropology student doing fieldwork in a remote part of the Khanuy Valley of Central Mongolia reported to the author that she observed people wearing blue jeans, baseball caps, and even a CVS Pharmacy T-shirt. Things like this should at least make the archaeologist pause when they find a Mississippian pottery sherd on a Late Prehistoric site.

The reader has now completed Archaeology 101 and 102 and will be happy to learn that there will not be a final exam. However, there is one final assignment. As you drive around the Falls area be aware of the various landscapes in the region because you now know their names, like the Scottsburg Lowland and the Knobs, and remember that for the last 10,000 years other people have also called this region their home.

Bibliography

Chapter 1

Justice, Noel
    1987 *Stone Age Spear and Arrow Points of the Midcontinental Eastern United States.* Indiana University Press (This is an excellent guide for classifying projectile points. It will only be referenced for Chapter 1, but it has been used in every chapter of this book in classifying projectile points.)

Chapter 2

Call, R. Ellsworth
    1896 Fishes and Shells of the Falls of the Ohio. In *Memorial History of Louisville from its First Settlement to the Year 1896*, Vol I, pp 13-17. Edited by J. Stoddard Johnston, Chicago. (An account from a naturalist who studied fish, mussels and snails at the Falls of the Ohio River.)

DeRegnaucourt, Tony and Jeff Georgiady
    1998 Prehistoric Chert Types of the Midwest. *Occasional Monographs Series of the Upper Miami Valley Archaeological Research Museum*, No.7, Greenville, Ohio. (This is an excellent book for anyone who wants a more detailed study of chert types used by Native Americans. The book contains color photographs and a detailed account of each type including; sources, color, texture, prehistoric utilization, and geographical distribution.)

Gunn, Charles R.
    1968 The Flora of Jefferson and Seven Adjacent Counties, Kentucky. *Annals of the Kentucky Society of Natural History*, Vol. 2. University of Louisville. (This may be the only publication that demonstrates that the Kentucky Scottsburg Lowland is a unique geological and botanical entity.)

Jackson, Daniel F.
    1962 Historical Notes on Fish Fauna, In, *Aquatic-Life Resources of the Ohio River*, pp. 5-13, Cincinnati. (This gives historic accounts of the numbers and kinds of fish in the Ohio River.)

Janzen, Donald E.
    1971 Excavations at the Falls of the Ohio River Region. *The Filson Club History Quarterly*, Vol. 45, No. 4, pp. 373-380. (This article gives radiocarbon dates from four sites in the Falls area and presents a classification of local cherts into six types. Since this publication was written Chert Type IV has been reclassified as a variety of Chert Type I.)

1977   An Examination of Late Archaic Development in the Falls of the Ohio River
       Area. In *For the Director: Research Essays in Honor of James B. Griffin*.
       Edited by Charles E. Cleland. *Museum of Anthropology, University of
       Michigan, Anthropological Papers* No. 61, pp. 123-143.   (This article discusses
       the geographical diversity in the Falls area, briefly describes eight sites in the
       area, and lists 20 radiocarbon dates.)

McFarlan, Arthur C.
   1961   *Geology of Kentucky*. The University of Kentucky, Lexington.

Powell, Richard L.
   1970   Geology of the Falls of the Ohio River. *State of Indiana Department of Natural
          Resources, Geological Survey* Circular No. 10. (This book presents a good
          description of the glacial origins of the Ohio River and the Falls.)

Schneider, Allan F.
   1966   Physiography. In Natural Features of Indiana. *Indiana Academy of Science*, pp. 40-
          56. Indianapolis.   (This article discusses the various geographical regions of
          Indiana with accompanying maps.)

Chapter 4

Knoblock, Byron W.
   1939   *Banner-Stones of the North American Indian*. Published by the author, LaGrange,
          Illinois.   (This highly illustrated book presents a classification of bannerstones and
          the evolution of their forms. It also includes results of experiments on the time
          needed to drill holes into various kinds of stone with a modern drill and a reed
          drill.)

Lutz, David L.
   2000   *The Archaic Bannerstone, Its Chronological History and Purpose, 6,000 B.C.-1,000
          B.C.*   Hynek Printing, Richland Center, Wisconsin. (An excellent book that goes
          beyond Knoblock's book in analyzing the bannerstone. Lutz questions the function
          of bannerstones as atlatl weights and suggests that they may have served as clan
          symbols.)

Matthews, James J.
   1958   Shell Mound Incised Bone and Stone Artifacts. *Ohio Archaeologist*, Vol.8, No.2, pp.
          42, 46. (This article pictures nine incised bone and two stone artifacts from the
          Clarksville site.)

Metraux, Alfred
   1949   Weapons. In *Handbook of South American Indians, The Comparative Ethnology
          of South American Indians,* edited by Julian H. Steward. *Bureau of American
          Ethnology*, Bulletin 153, Vol. 5, pp. 229-263 Washington. (Metraux uses the term
          "spear thrower" instead of "atlatl" and mentions its use in over twenty-five tribes in

Columbia, Brazil, Peru, Ecuador, Argentina, and gives descriptions. None have an Atlatl weight. See pages 244-247)

Perkins, William R. "Atlatl Bob"
1992   Stealth Technology 1992 BC. *Bulletin of Primitive Technology*, Issue #4. ("Atlatl Bob" has devoted his life to studying the atlatl and this article questions some of the myth surrounding bannerstones and presents evidence why a weight is needed on an atlatl.)

Priegel, G.R.
1967   The Freshwater Drum - Its Life, History, Ecology and Management. *Wisconsin Department of Natural Resources*, Publication 236. (Gives good information on the habitat of the freshwater drum.)

Webb, Clarence H.
1968   The Extent and Content of Poverty Point Culture. *American Antiquity*, Vol. 33, No. 3, pp. 297-321. (The Poverty Point Objects found at the Clarksville site are mentioned in this article on page 307. Other sites where Poverty Point Objects have been found are also reported.)

Webb, Wm. S.
1946   Indian Knoll - Site Oh 2, Ohio County, Kentucky. *Reports in Anthropology and Archaeology*, Volume IV, Number 3, Part 1. Department of Anthropology and Archaeology, University of Kentucky, Lexington. (On pages 159-168 there is a section on atlatls found in association with burials and photographs of twelve burials are shown. There is a discussion of the atlatl on pages 319-333. This is one of the earliest works that shows the association of the atlatl, weight, and hook.)

Witt, Arthur, Jr.
1960   Length and Weight of Ancient Freshwater Drum, *Aplodinotus grunniens*, Calculated from Otoliths Found in Indian Middens. *Copia*, 1960, No.3, pp. 181-185. (This brief article gives the equation for calculating the length or weight of the freshwater drum based on the length or weight of an otolith.)

Chapter 5

Bader, Anne Tobbe
1992   An Analysis of Bone and Antler Tools Use Patterns from the Kentucky Air National Guard Site. Master's Thesis, Department of Anthropology, University of Kentucky, Lexington. (Besides an excellent analysis of the bone and antler tools from the KYANG site, this thesis gives a good description of other artifacts and faunal remains found on the site.) Note: Permission was given by the author of this thesis to use Figure 6.16. Modifications to this figure were made in terms of realigning the artifacts and adding descriptive text. These modifications were reviewed and approved by the author of the thesis.

Bader, Anne Tobbe and Joseph E. Granger
1989   Recent Archaeological Investigations on the Kentucky Air National Guard Site,
       (15JF267) Jefferson County, Kentucky. (This is the final report of excavations at the
       KYANG site submitted by Granger Consultants to the Kentucky Air National Guard.
       The number of artifacts, chert waste flakes, mammal and fish bone, and shells
       recovered from the site was taken from this publication. Salt River Side Notched
       points are shown in Figure VIII-1, page VIII-3).

Burnett, Richard
1963   Lone Hill. *Central States Archaeological Journal*, Vol. 10, No. 3, pp.84-90. (This is
       probably the first published article on the Lone Hill site and it is based on an
       account by Eugene Atherton who was one of the first people to collect from the
       site.)

Collins, Lewis
1878   *History of Kentucky*, Vol. II (revised edition). Collins & Company, Covington. (A
       discussion of the iron ores of Bullitt County is found on page 101)

Granger, Joseph E.
1988   Late/Terminal Archaic Settlement in the Falls of the Ohio River Region of Kentucky:
       An Examination of Components, Phases and Clusters. In *Paleoindian and Archaic
       Research in Kentucky*, pp. 153-203. Edited by Charles D. Hockensmith, David
       Pollack, and Thomas Sanders. Kentucky Heritage Council. (Granger mentions a
       number of sites in the Falls area including Lone Hill and Minors Lane. The KYANG
       site is discussed in detail and presents much of the information found in the 1989
       publication by Bader and Granger.)

Hardaway, Howard
1941   "Out of the Wet Woods Come Towering Stories". *The Courier- Journal*, June 8.
       (This article recounts stories of early settlers about the Wet Woods.)

Matthews, James J.
1963   Archaic Cache from Jefferson County, Kentucky. *Ohio Archaeologist*, Vol.13, No.1,
       pp.6-7. (This article describes the cache of three axes and bannerstone found by
       the author at the Calhoun site.   This is the site that later became known as the
       Minors Lane site. The article also included a photograph of the cache.)

Chapter 6

Lutz, David L.
2000   *The Archaic Bannerstone, Its Chronological History and Purpose, 6,000 B.C. - 1,000
       B.C.* Hynek Printing, Richland Center, Wisconsin. (Although the subject of this
       book is bannerstones, there is a brief discussion (pages 368-371)of Archaic stone
       cups and there are photographs of eleven whole cups.

Wagers, Charlie
    1991   Limestone Shotcups. *Prehistoric American*, Vol. XXV, No.2, p.20 (This is a one-page article on stone cups with a photograph of a cup found at a site on the Ohio River.)

Chapter 7

Matthews, James J.
    1958   The Zorn Avenue Village Site, Jefferson County, Louisville, Kentucky. *Ohio Archaeologist*, Vol.8, No.4, pp. 114-126. (This article pictures and describes stone artifacts from the Zorn Avenue site.)

Mocas, Stephen T.
    1988   Pinched and Punctated Pottery of the Falls of the Ohio River Region: A Reappraisal of the Zorn Punctate Ceramic Type. In *New Deal Era Archaeology and Current Research in Kentucky*, edited by David Pollack and Mary Lucas Powell, pp.115-142. Kentucky Heritage Council. (Mocas is the authority on the pottery from the Zorn Avenue site. This publication is a detailed study of Zorn Punctate and a comparison with other pinched-design pottery from Kentucky and neighboring states.)

    1992   Falls Plain: A Middle Woodland Ceramic Type from the Falls of the Ohio River Region. In *Current Archaeological Research in Kentucky: Volume Two*, edited by David Pollack and Gwynn Henderson, pp. 55-78. Kentucky Heritage Council. (This excellent article presents a detailed analysis of the pottery type Falls Plain.)

Webb, Wm. S. And Charles E. Snow
    1945   The Adena People. *Reports in Anthropology and Archaeology*, Volume VI, Department of Anthropology and Archaeology, University of Kentucky, Lexington. (This is a summary of excavations of Adena sites conducted by the University of Kentucky.)

Chapter 8

Haag, William G.
    1942   The Pottery from the C and O Mounds at Paintsville. In *The C and O Mounds at Paintsville*, by Wm. S. Webb. *Reports in Anthropology and Archaeology*, Volume V, No. 4, pp.341-349, Department of Anthropology and Archaeology, University of Kentucky, Lexington. (Haag mentions sand tempered plain pottery from the C and O mounds and suggests the classification Woodland Plain as a type to cover the Various types of Early Woodland plain ceramics.)

Janzen, Donald E.
    2004   Ceramics from the Muddy Fork Site in Jefferson County, Kentucky. *Currents of Change*, Vol 2, No.2, pp.57-68. (This article presents a detailed discussion of the analysis of Muddy Fork ceramics.)

Chapter 9

Holmberg, Allan
    1948   The Siriono. In *Handbook of South American Indians, The Tropical Forest Tribes,*
           edited by Julian H. Steward *Bureau of American Ethnology*, Bulletin 143, Vol. 3,
           pp.455-463. Washington. (Holmberg discusses the size of bands on page 458.)

Lepper, Bradley T.
    2005   *Ohio Archaeology: An Illustrtated Chronicle of Ohio's Ancient American Indian
           Cultures.* Orange Frazer Press. (This book devotes an entire chapter to the Late
           Prehistoric period and gives some of the defining characteristics.)

Milner, George R.
    2004   *The Moundbuilders: Ancient Peoples of Eastern North America.* Thanes & Hudson
           (A very readable book with a good presentation on the Late Woodland and
           Mississippian periods.)

Pollack, David and A. Gwynn Herderson
    2000   Late Woodland Cultures in Kentucky. *Late Woodland Societies: Tradition and
           Transformation across the Midcontinent*, edited by Thomas E. Emerson, Dale L.
           McElrath, & Andrew C. Fortier, pp. 613-641. (An excellent article presenting the
           argument that the Falls of the Ohio River was the intersection of upstream and
           downstream cultures during Late Woodland times.)

Spencer, Robert F.
    1959   The North Alansan Eskimo: A Study in Ecology and Society. *Smithsonian Institution
           Bureau of American Ethnology*, Bulletin 171. Government Printing Office,
           Washington.   (A discussion of Tareumiut settlement patterns and people remaining
           at the main village year-round can be found on pp. 140-145. The size of seasonal
           and base camps are given on pages 132-139.

Spencer, Robert F., Jesse D. Jennings, et. al.
    1965   *The Native Americans.* Harper & Row Publishers. (Chapter III in this book,
           "Language - American Babel" has been used to get information on Native American
           languages.)